SOAS Since the Sixties

edited by
David Arnold and Christopher Shackle

Published by the School of Oriental and African Studies (University of London)
Thornhaugh Street, Russell Square, London, WC1H 0XG

© School of Oriental and African Studies, 2003

British Library Cataloguing in Publication Data
A catalogue record for this book is available from the British Library

ISBN 0 7286 0353 5

Designed by Hawksmere Printed in Great Britain by Bookcraft

Preface

This idea of this volume arose around the turn of the millennium with the realization that the School was rapidly approaching its centenary in 2017 without any serious thought having been given to the updating of its history beyond Sir Cyril Philips's brief account which had been published for its fiftieth anniversary in 1967. It was originally intended to commission a comprehensive institutional history from a single author. When this plan fell through, it was decided to go for the present format of an edited volume incorporating individually authored chapters. The notes on contributors at the end of the book indicate their often remarkable length of service throughout the period 1967-2002 which is covered. As is suggested by the title, *SOAS Since the Sixties* is therefore in a real sense the first-hand record of a generation of academics who together have seen the School through a period of great change. One day, perhaps, it may play its part as a source for that fuller history which the centenary of SOAS will deserve. In the meantime it is hoped that our collective account will entertain as well as instruct all those interested in the development of one of the world's most remarkable and distinctive university institutions.

A collective undertaking of this kind has relied for its successful completion upon the good will and helpfulness of a number of colleagues. While themselves assuming due responsibility for the final shape of the volume, the editors wish to thank all contributors for their willing cooperation. We are particularly grateful to Frank Dabell for his encouragement of the project, to Professor Tony Allan for his generous help in drawing up the second section of our Introduction which is based on his earlier draft, to Helen Cordell and to all those who have advised or commented on earlier drafts of individual chapters. We also wish to express our thanks to Martin Daly for his invaluable assistance with the editorial process and to Michael Sherry for his enthusiastic oversight of the volume's production.

David Arnold
Christopher Shackle

Contents

List of illustrations

Colour illustrations

Illustrations in text

1

Introduction: SOAS at the crossroads

David Arnold and Christopher Shackle

A bumpy ride

Nearly four decades have elapsed since Professor C. H. Philips, the then Director of the School of Oriental and African Studies, wrote his brief history of the School's first fifty years. Since the mid-1960s SOAS has undergone an immense transformation, as great as any that Philips himself effected and recorded. That transformation has been impelled by many factors – by the legacy of Philips's own vision of a dynamic and rejuvenated SOAS, by seismic shifts in government policy towards university organization, accountability and funding, by dramatic increases in student numbers and the physical expansion of the School, by the decline in the authority of the University of London and the growing autonomy of its colleges, by the evolving nature of our academic disciplines and the shifting institutional balance between them. Many of these changes have been imposed upon the School, in common with other higher education institutions in Britain, but they have affected it in distinct ways that are themselves worthy of record. Simply to have survived from the depleted position in which the School found itself in the early 1980s deserves commemoration. To have done so with vigour, imagination and a renewed vision of SOAS's distinctive place among UK universities and colleges and in the wider world of global academe calls for a real celebration.

At a time when the School is witnessing a renewed period of major change – signalled by the opening of the Vernon Square campus in 2001 and the move to a Faculty structure in 2002 – the opening years of the twenty-first century seem an appropriate and opportune moment to reflect on how the School has changed and on the upheavals it has endured since the mid-1960s. It is also a time when many of those who witnessed and contributed to the transformation of the last forty years have recently left the School or are about to retire from its service. As well as being an institutional record, this volume is thus something of a collective personal memoir of those years. It is hoped that this survey of *SOAS Since the Sixties* will also serve as an introductory guide to those who have only lately come to know the School or who, approaching it for the first time as outsiders, want to know more about why and how SOAS has come to be the kind of place that it now is.

The modern shape of the School was first decisively defined by Sir Cyril Philips, its Director from 1957 to 1976. His account of the history of SOAS up to 1967, summarized by David Arnold in the opening chapter of this volume, shows how SOAS passed through several crises of identity and growth in its first fifty years. The sheer breadth of Philips's vision for the School remains remarkable, embracing as it did a strategic academic expansion into social sciences and into area studies, the foundation of an overdue growth in student numbers, the careful alignment of SOAS with then generous policies of university funding, the targeted solicitation of external benefactions, and the construction of the major building which houses the School's unique Library at its core and which is now rightly named the Philips Building.

The following chapter by Richard Rathbone carries down to the present the story of the School's Directors, Secretaries and other senior office holders whose names are listed at the end the book. Rathbone's chapter too bears witness to Philips's achievements, before showing how the School has continued to endure some extremely difficult times, not least in the drastic staff cuts made during the early 1980s when Professor Jeremy Cowan was Director. The loss to the School in terms of experienced academic staff and, no less, of morale and sense of purpose was considerable. In 1967, when SOAS was still the beneficiary of the combined largess of the 1946 Scarbrough Report and the 1961 Hayter Report (into which Philips himself had had a notable input), the number of academic staff had stood at 227. This had fallen to 165 twenty years later, and it was only with the 1986 Parker Report that a gradual recovery began. This recovery was in part conducted according to the strategic blueprint set out in what remains the most comprehensive internal review the School has ever undertaken, the 1982 Report of the Working Party on Longer-term Development which was established by Cowan with Malcolm Yapp as Chair. But, despite such setbacks and adversities as those experienced in the early 1980s, SOAS did more than survive, and in the 1990s under the enterprising Directorship of Michael McWilliam and with the progressive devolution by the University of London of most of its powers to its constituent colleges it entered into a new phase of increasingly independent growth and vitality.

The story of the successful development during the period from 1967 to 2002 of the School's very varied academic portfolio in the face of diverse and often difficult challenges is told from three different perspectives in the three chapters by Christopher Shackle, J. D. Y. Peel and Terence J. Byres. Respectively covering the language and culture departments, the arts and humanities and the social sciences, and inevitably giving much attention to the minute measuring of departmental staff numbers which is so engrained in the dons' eye view of the world, these parallel chapters show how SOAS has been able to shift an ever greater allocation of resources to the social sciences in keeping with changing student demands without sacrificing the core of its internationally recognized strengths in the languages of Asia and Africa.

For an institution of its size and resources, the School can fairly be said to have maintained a formidable battery of academic activities and initiatives. And yet it cannot be denied that SOAS continues to be beset by a number of seemingly intractable problems. Some of these are generic to higher education in Britain in the late twentieth and early twenty-first centuries; but others are specific to SOAS as (despite its recent growth) a relatively small academic institution which has a highly distinctive specialized mission for Asian and African studies.

One manifestation of the particular character of SOAS is the proportion of its resources which has always been needed to maintain the exceptional institutional prominence of its Library, which is itself so important a part of the Philips legacy. As Keith Webster and Rosemary Seton show in their chapter, the SOAS Library has long since established its importance as a national and international academic resource, and it has also been the basis for several successful funding initiatives in recent years. It is an occasional cause for rueful pride that the SOAS Library has sometimes been better known and more fully utilized by outsiders than have the teaching and research activities of the School itself. And yet, by the very nature of its specialization, the Library, including its increasingly large collection of archives, has been an expensive asset for the School to maintain at the same time as increased student numbers make ever greater demands for the support of the Library's teaching collections.

The difficulty of reconciling expansion in terms both of student numbers and of academic research agendas with a central London location, where new space is physically and financially hard to come by, is detailed in Frank Dabell's chapter on the School's estate. But it has been symptomatic of how SOAS has emerged

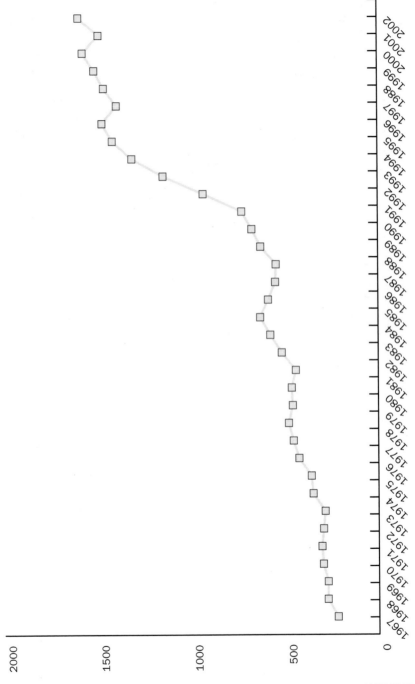

undergraduate student numbers 1967-2002

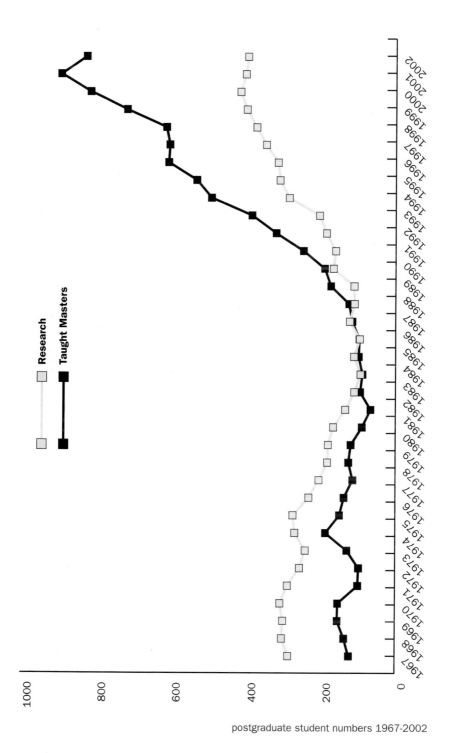

postgraduate student numbers 1967-2002

positively and purposefully from the low point of the early 1980s that it has managed to expand from its original building designed in the 1930s and the Library building added to it in the 1970s to develop into something more akin to a campus university. The importance of this physical growth in the School's estate is highlighted by Richard Rathbone in his assessment of the role of the School's recent Directors and Secretaries, as well as by Frank Dabell, whose own contribution to these developments has been quite crucial. The building of the Brunei Gallery, the creation of two new halls of residence and the acquisition of the Vernon Square building to allow for the growth in both teaching and administrative needs has brought about the most evident and physically obvious transformation in the School's recent history. This physical expansion is set to continue with the current development of the East Block and the long overdue internal refurbishment of the main entrance to match the increasingly leafy Thornhaugh Street outside which provides the School with such welcome outdoor social space.

The greatest of the main problems which SOAS has had to face has undoubtedly been that of size. As anyone who has known it will be aware, even over the past decade or two the School has grown enormously. Looking back on Sir Cyril Philips's account of the first fifty years of the School, one cannot but be astonished by the tiny number of degree students taught at SOAS even as late as the early 1960s. Undergraduate numbers have since then increased by leaps and bounds, especially since the mid-1990s (see the accompanying tables on pp.4-5); so have the number of Masters students, stimulated initially by the creation of Area Studies MAs in the 1960s, but more recently through a diverse array of attractive disciplinary programmes in such fields as Economics and Development Studies. In 2000-01, the total number of students at SOAS rose above 3,000 for the first time. Remarkably (and the figure itself suggests something of the distinctive nature of SOAS), of this total nearly 50 per cent were postgraduate students: in 2000-01 SOAS had 1,515 undergraduates, 1,316 postgraduates, plus 441 other students registered for special programmes and diplomas. A further 1,302 postgraduates were registered as studying through part-time distance education, itself a significant development of recent years and one that augurs well for the future. Despite the difficulties that resulted for the School from the Government-imposed increase in overseas student fees in the late 1970s, SOAS has continued to attract significant numbers of students from outside the UK and particularly from outside the European Union: in 2000-01 29 per cent of undergraduate and postgraduate students were from outside the EU, particularly from Asian countries.

It is striking, however, that despite the tenfold increase in student numbers over the past forty years, academic staff numbers at SOAS today do not greatly exceed those of the seemingly halcyon Hayter years: in 2002-03 the School had an academic staff of 247 (as against 227 in 1967) and there is little likelihood of this increasing significantly in the coming years. To no small extent, it has only been possible for the School to continue to provide for expanding numbers of students, and the exacting demands of government-driven accountability which at times threaten almost to overwhelm with administrative tasks a relatively small institution like SOAS, by augmenting the complement of non-academic staff not only in the Registry, but also in the Estates, Finance, Human Resources, Information Technology, Marketing and Research departments and, since the summer of 2002, in the new Faculty offices. Though this inevitably gives rise to tensions of its own, especially among those academics who feel that all possible funding should be directed to serve teaching and research needs, in the twenty-first century the importance of administrative and support staff to the viability and efficiency of higher education institutions has grown far beyond anything that could have been envisaged in the first fifty years of the School.

The changing experiences of SOAS students as their numbers have grown over the decades, and the growth and professionalization of the administration which provides the essential underpinning which supports all the activities of an increasingly complex institution, are not given the explicit attention which each deserves in this volume. But some of the continuities which have helped to characterize SOAS and to hold it together as a place with the most extraordinary ability to capture the imagination and the loyalty of so many who have come into contact with it are set out in the personal memoir by Hugh Baker with which the book ends. Himself first a student at the School in the 1950s, then a long serving member of the academic staff throughout the period covered by this book before retiring as an administrator, few are as well qualified as Hugh to articulate the spirit of SOAS.

Redesigning SOAS: The centres approach

Apart from issues of size, a further, and abiding, issue at SOAS, highlighted in several of the following contributions, is how far the School should see itself as a congeries of groupings based upon the geographical areas of study, traditionally divided at SOAS between the five regions of East Asia, South East Asia, South Asia, the Middle

East, and Africa, or as adhering primarily to a teaching and research structure based upon the academic disciplines which have become increasingly important in defining national criteria for the organization and support of teaching and research.

So far as the disciplines within the School's remit are concerned, several new departments have come into being as part of the general process of expansion and diversification that has characterized SOAS since the early 1960s. As Professors Peel and Byres show in their chapters in this volume, the period since the early 1960s has seen the creation and growth of new departments in both arts and social sciences at SOAS, and there has been a more general shift in the School's orientation in terms of both staff and student numbers away from the language and culture departments towards the social sciences and arts. Among the recent additions to the muster-roll of SOAS departments have been Art and Archaeology (1990), Study of Religions (1992), Development Studies (1995), Music (1998), and, most recently of all, the Department of Financial and Management Studies in 2002, while only Geography has ceased to be with the transfer of the SOAS department to King's College in 2001. The School can now boast having sixteen departments compared to a modest eleven in 1968.

An important parallel development at SOAS since the early 1960s, and one not otherwise recounted in these pages, has been the creation and growth alongside academic departments of regional and 'special purpose' centres. The idea of regional centres owed much to the stimulus of the Hayter Report of 1961, which recommended the creation of area studies centres in British universities. A number of successful bids for funding were made under this scheme, including Middle Eastern studies at Oxford and Durham, South East Asian Studies at Hull, West African Studies at Birmingham and South Asian Studies at Cambridge. At the time SOAS did not feel the need to create area studies centres of its own, believing that in its language and culture departments it already had an area studies profile. However, Philips became increasing concerned that SOAS appeared to be losing out on this important initiative and the funding associated with it. He alluded to this in the School's *Annual Report* for 1958-59 in recognizing the need to increase departmental, but more especially interdisciplinary, research, and in his review of the 1957-62 quinquennium he further spoke of the value of using Masters degrees as a means of attracting to Asian and African studies students whose previous work had been confined to Europe.

In his introduction to the 1961-62 *Annual Report*, Philips further regretted the School's failure to make provision for 'modern studies'. Finally, in the 1965-66 session he announced his intention to set up area studies centres at SOAS, in part as a vehicle for the kinds of interdisciplinary studies that Hayter funding had made possible elsewhere and to allow for the development of area studies Masters programmes. Philips feared that because area studies centres elsewhere had regional labels attached to them, they were seen in many quarters as being *the* national centres for the study of those areas, even though SOAS already had far larger provision for them than anywhere else. He had hoped to establish a special relationship with those centres, as part of a national division of labour, with SOAS providing the language teaching, the postgraduate supervision and library support. But it soon became apparent that competition, not co-operation, was to be the order of the day and that SOAS was losing out in the battle for both recognition and funding.

As a result, between 1966 and 1968, five Area Centres came into being at SOAS – for Africa, the Near and Middle East, South Asia, South East Asia and what was then called the Far East. All members of academic staff were expected to belong to one of these regional centres, which, crucially, were intended to complement, but not to replace, the existing departmental structure. The first Centre Chairs were chosen from among the more senior academic figures in the School – Roland Oliver for Africa, Taki Vatikiotis for the Middle East, Adrian Mayer for South Asia, Jeremy Cowan for South East Asia, and William Beasley for the Far East. Given their stature in the School and international reputations, they were able to launch the Centres with considerable flair and success. Seminars were begun, conferences held, and internationally renowned speakers invited to speak at the School.

Identifying a second generation of leadership proved more difficult, however, and indeed finding able and willing Centre Chairs (who are also likely to be in demand as Heads and other departmental officers, such as admission tutors) has been over the past forty years one of the continuing problems facing the Centres. The Chair initially served a term of four years (later reduced to three) and each of the original Centres has been served by ten or eleven Chairs since the mid-1960s, a heavy call on the services of academic staff. Some departments seem to have been decidedly cool towards the Area Centres and to have discouraged their members from becoming Chairs. Others, notably History and Anthropology, have provided a high proportion of Centre leadership. The performance of Centre Chairs has varied enormously over the years: some have been less active and imaginative than others; a hardworking few have managed to keep the profile of the Area Centres high not only in terms of internal School activity but also in the minds of the wider academic community and the general public. Many academics at the School continue to see the Centres as having an indispensable role.

In the early years Centre Chairs were given a place on leading School committees, including an expanded Heads of Departments Committee and the Research Committee, and if this added to their responsibilities it also enhanced their status within the School structure. However, the School was generally reluctant to commit substantial resources to the Centres and with each financial crisis the resources available to them were pared down: from having once had their own secretaries and offices in the 1970s, most by the 1990s found themselves having to share with other Centres. Despite the early optimism, SOAS has found it increasingly difficult to manage both a Departmental and an Area Centre structure and the cumulative pressures of Government teaching and research assessment exercises have further favoured prioritizing departments over Centres.

One of the most important contributions made by the Area Centres was in Masters teaching. In the 1960s the area studies approach was not regarded as a suitable framework for undergraduate teaching, but was thought to be ideal for the training of Masters students who already had a first-degree foundation in a specific disciplinary field. The area studies Masters degrees were introduced in 1966-68 at a time when existing Masters programmes attracted very few students. Between the 1970s and 1990s they proved a remarkable success. In that period area studies Masters programmes accounted for roughly 70 percent of all Masters students at SOAS, passing 70 in 1975 and then, after a series of setbacks (due mainly to the international situation), rising to over 150 in 1995-96. After 1989, however, it was degrees in such discipline-based fields as Anthropology, Development Studies, Economics and Law which began to make up the bulk of Masters enrolments, and which lifted total numbers to over 560 in 1996-97. By that date the proportion of area studies Masters students (which were no longer directly linked to the Area Centres) had fallen to 18 percent of the total, although still numbering about one hundred per year. In this respect, as in many others, SOAS, in order to survive and to flourish, has had to be flexible and pragmatic.

A further difficulty with the initial Area Centres approach of the mid-1960s has been one of subdivision. Having five regional Centres proved not to be enough. The Far East (a term displaced by East Asia at SOAS in the 1980s) rapidly split into two separate Centres – one for China, the other for Japan – and in June 1968

Stuart Schram created the Contemporary China Institute to bring academic vigour to the study of modern China. The more recent growth of area specialisms and related funding opportunities have since led to the creation of a separate centre for Korean Studies, a field generously supported at SOAS by the Korea Foundation, and in 2000 for Central Asia, following the award to the School of additional posts concerned with this region. In place of the original five, there are thus currently eight Area Centres at SOAS: the Centre of African Studies, the Centre of Middle Eastern Studies, the Centre of Chinese Studies (now incorporating the Contemporary China Institute), the Centre of Contemporary Central Asia and the Caucasus, the Centre of South Asian Studies, the Centre of South East Asian Studies, the Japan Research Centre and the Centre of Korean Studies. There also exist at SOAS a number of smaller, less formally recognized groupings, as for instance for Turkish Studies, which have never been officially elevated to the status of Centres.

Moreover, the area studies concept, so fashionable in the 1960s and 1970s as a way of combining interdisciplinary expertise on a wide geographical region, has lost some of its impetus four decades later. Quite a number of SOAS academics today do not have a strong commitment to any one of the established regions: some, especially in the social sciences, have a far stronger disciplinary than regional focus; a few work mainly on areas like Latin America that lie outside the old SOAS remit. There has been a growth in more specific areas of interest, some of which cut across the old Area Studies regions or which entail more specialized areas of study within a given region. Some of these have become departments in their own right, while others have been recognized as 'special purposes centres' with primary ties to departments (and now Faculties) rather than to regional Centres. The list of these newer centres is now a long one, but it includes such distinctive fields as Buddhist Studies, Islamic and Middle Eastern Law, Gender and Religions, and Jewish Studies, and in terms of seminar programmes, conferences, research, fundraising and outreach to the wider community, these include some of the most active and energetic groupings in the School, as well as allowing for more flexibility than the Area Centres have tended to permit. In taking stock of this richly diverse growth in its report to Academic Board of 1999, a working party recommended the encouragement of these newer Centres while seeing a particular role for the Area Centres in continuing to represent the important regional dimension of the School's external profile.

Managing growth

The growth in student numbers has been an essential part of the School's finances in recent years: in 2000-01 £15.2 million of the total income of £38.2 million came from tuition fee income. But in the increasingly complex financial situation in which universities now find themselves, SOAS has also had to look for other sources of income to sustain even its core activities. The handouts from departments of state, colonial governments and seemingly small sums of money gleaned from the Universities Grants Commission, as described by Philips, look paltry by today's standards; and SOAS, in common with other London Schools and Colleges, no longer receives the major part of its income through the Senate House of the University of London. Grants from the universities' current paymaster, the Higher Education Funding Council for England (HEFCE), for such areas of performance as the periodic Research Assessment Exercise (RAE), accounted in 2000-01 for a further £11 million of the School's income. But, such are the rapid variations of Government policy with which universities now have somehow to contend, that the RAE as a major source of SOAS income is now seriously under threat.

Again, as is described in Christopher Shackle's account of the language departments at SOAS, the School has over the years been heavily dependent for what many justly continue to regard as key areas of its activity on exceptional Government provision, the so-called 'special factor' or 'minority subjects' funding. Following on in the tradition of the Scarbrough and Hayter Reports, the School's unique contribution to teaching and research on the languages of Asia and Africa was recognized by the Parker Report of 1986 and by its successors, the Raisman Report of 1993 and the Minority Subjects Report in 2000. In addition, especially as the Government contribution to university funding in Britain has proportionately declined, the School has also been sustained by outside grants and by the individual donations, some of them remarkably generous like the endowment of the Brunei Gallery or the recent establishment of the Endangered Languages Programme by the Lisbet Rausing Charitable Fund.

SOAS has also been sustained by the property sales described by Frank Dabell in his chapter on the School's estate, which have helped SOAS to meet an annual expenditure now in excess of £30 million a year. But, as the experience of 2002-03 has once again shown with its fresh talk of financial crisis, it remains a constant struggle to maintain viability in an institution that lacks the kinds of ancient endowments that help to support some leading universities in Britain and abroad, and which is without the large science, technology and medicine departments that often attract large research funding and that tend to enjoy a privileged place in Government thinking. SOAS is certainly not alone in needing to devote an increasing proportion of its resources and the time of its Director and other senior administrative staff to fund-raising and related income-generating activities, at the cost of other important tasks; but, given the School's distinctive remit, this has created exceptional difficulties of its own.

And yet, it is as well to remind ourselves that, for all this remarkable pattern of recent growth, making SOAS a very different kind of a place from what it was in the 1960s, as Hugh Baker shows from his personal recollection of the School over several decades, it remains in current UK terms a relatively small institution. Its student numbers are dwarfed by those of its near neighbours, most obviously University College and Imperial College, and in terms of its annual turnover, its research income and fundraising, it remains small compared to the UK's academic giants. Despite the 'campus feel' that SOAS has acquired with the Brunei building, the residences and Vernon Square, the School is still short of space for teaching, administration and research. It is certainly a justifiable cause for pride that SOAS, while remaining true to its specialist mission, has steadily outgrown such institutions as the School of Slavonic and East European Studies (SSEES), founded as a sister institution within the University in 1916 but now wholly incorporated into UCL, or smaller University of London bodies like the Institute of Commonwealth Studies or the Institute of Latin American Studies, each occupying no more than a single terrace building in Bloomsbury. But in an academic environment that seems increasingly to favour larger institutions, it is a constant struggle for a smallish SOAS to survive.

But is being relatively small such a disadvantage? There are those academics and visitors, from Britain and abroad, who continue to welcome the relatively small size of the School – the greater freedom of communication it can allow between staff and students or across regional and disciplinary fields that might elsewhere be hived off into physically separate locations. SOAS still has a feeling of intimacy and immediacy, a kind of collective buzz, that many other higher education institutions in this country and around the world have lost or were never fortunate enough ever to have had. However, while student numbers have grown, the physical confines of SOAS have expanded, and the volume of teaching and research has increased exponentially, the number of permanent academic staff, as we have seen, has not greatly increased over that reached in the Philips era. The increased pressures on academic time and energy are common to the UK higher education sector as a whole, but they press particularly hard upon a smallish institution which has so little room for physical growth and flexibility, and where, as Richard Rathbone shows, there have been great expectations not only in terms of teaching and research, but also of commitments to administration in a relatively large number of departments and centres as well as across the School as a whole. Following the removal of the former binary divide between universities and polytechnics in 1992, there has been an ever more intense struggle for competition and survival among UK higher education institutions and this has recently resulted in an apparent trend towards mergers: the recent history of University College, including its absorption of SSEES, provides one model, close at hand, of how academic expansion can lead to the disappearance of vulnerable smaller institutions. SOAS has thus far successfully avoided a merger or takeover, and should be proud of its continuing independence and its ability, in often highly adverse circumstances, to continue to attract good students at all levels, to develop its estate imaginatively and to boost its income from research grants and private donations.

It is a tribute to the loyalty and commitment SOAS commands among its staff and students, that the idea of close association with University College or indeed any other London college or university has hitherto been resisted, with a widespread sense, it might be said, that beggary in Bloomsbury is preferable to being swallowed up in a larger, more amorphous university. Paradoxically, however, SOAS often finds it collectively difficult to be more bullish about its own identity and achievements, and to measure itself positively against the country's academic giants. Areas of collaboration with other institutions remain relatively limited or undeveloped, but will certainly need to be explored more actively in future. Equally, however, any substantial dilution of the long-established regional and disciplinary identity of the School would rightly be resisted. So perhaps for the present SOAS's destiny is sealed – as a smallish but vibrant institution wedded to a rather specific mission of its own.

The dilemmas of SOAS

As Sir Cyril Philips's opening chapter clearly shows, the School has always been torn between two different, possibly conflicting, roles. On the one hand, it has seen itself as a practically minded institution, providing language instruction or offering courses of vocational value to outside individuals and organizations. In this SOAS was perhaps better attuned than many of its counterparts to now current government expectations of universities' roles in the modern world. The School's central London location has always been a factor in its practical, this-worldly orientation, and that ill-informed and dismissive term often applied to UK universities of being 'ivory towers' has generally seemed an even less meaningful description of SOAS (especially perhaps since the construction of the gaunt concrete of the Philips Building!) than of institutions located in remote fenlands, in declining county towns, or on bucolic green-field sites. These days part of this practical, service-oriented, role has been removed from the main departmental activity of the School and entrusted to the Language Centre, whose delivery of non-degree training in Asian and African languages to a great variety of users drawn from government, business and the community has expanded greatly in recent years under the leadership of Ulrich Kratz, and to the Briefings Office which is now known as SOAS Interface and is currently overseen by Professor Hugh Baker. The successful development led by Sue Yates in providing attractive and professionally run introductory courses and programmes for overseas students through what is now designated IFCELS (International Foundation Courses and English Language Studies) has been one of the rather unsung achievements of recent years, but its crucial contribution to the independence of the School will certainly command the attention of any future historian of the period.

Especially since the end of the Second World War and the Scarbrough and Hayter Reports, SOAS has been determined to develop and maintain its reputation as a leading scholarly institution, with a high teaching and research profile of its own. In this respect the School has gained in confidence and public recognition since the start of the Philips era over fifty years ago. It has unquestionably established itself as one of the UK's leading institutions, especially (but not exclusively) with respect to the study and understanding of Asia and Africa, to an extent that could barely have been anticipated in the 1930s or 1940s. However, part of the enduring SOAS dilemma is how far it should continue to trade on its identity as a 'specialist', regionally specific institution. As several of the chapters in this history demonstrate, there have been a number of profound changes in the nature and orientation of the School since the 1960s. One has been the move away from the 'classical' tradition of Oriental and African scholarship (as identified by Christopher Shackle in his chapter), towards the growth of the social sciences (as Terry Byres shows), and this trend is clearly set to continue. Starting from the Philips years, there has been a parallel shift away from pre-modern historical and literary studies towards greater engagement with the contemporary world to the extent that even the History Department and the language and culture departments now have a clear majority of academic staff engaged in teaching and research relating to the modern world, mostly specializing in the post-1900 world. This, too, is a trend that is likely to continue, but it would be a pity, whatever student demand and state funding might favour, to see SOAS lose its standing as a centre for 'classical' learning.

Looking back at the early history of the School, one can only be struck by how far its concerns were located in the study of, and associated practice within, societies located 'out there' in time as well as in space. The origins of the School as a place for the instruction of trainee civil servants, missionaries, businessmen and wartime servicemen reinforced the underlying sense of serving, intellectually as well as administratively, the needs of an overseas empire. The loss of that empire and the emergence of a multi-racial society in Britain have gradually encouraged SOAS to rethink its role. It remains, of course, a central part of the School's work in teaching and research to look beyond the confines of Britain and Europe and to help shed light on the nature of Asian and African societies. But increasingly the old division between 'here' and 'out there' has broken down and the ethnic composition of the School, teachers and students alike, and the move away from a certain type of 'Oriental' studies has allowed the School to think more freely about its contribution to the study of the languages and cultures of Asia and Africa as they operate in twenty-first century Britain and about the diasporic communities that have transformed British society in ways which even in the days of the Scarbrough and Hayter Reports went largely unconsidered. It is ironic (if salutary) that at a time when, in the wake of Edward Said's work, the very idea of 'Orientalism' as a legitimate realm of scholarly pursuit has been subjected to sustained critique, there has never been more need for an intelligent attempt to nurture such understanding and to value what brings diverse societies and cultures together as well as to comprehend that which tears them apart.

To this aspect of the School's gradual intellectual reorientation may further be linked the significant changes that have taken place within the University of London itself. As the first fifty years of the School showed, SOAS managed over the course of several decades to establish itself in the then prized position of being a college of the University, with corresponding recognition for its degree courses and with funding routed in large part through Senate House. One of the consequences of this arrangement was that SOAS thought of itself as essentially part of that wider academic entity, with a remit to offer specialized teaching and research into the parts of the world that other colleges did not reach. It was, in effect, a small section of a huge departmental store, in which other parts of the academic enterprise stocked all the things that SOAS did not. This had the benefit of carving out for the School a seemingly secure, distinctive, and largely regionally defined role of its own. One disadvantage of this arrangement was that while SOAS benefited from the overall prestige of the University and from some of its administrative functions, it was also restricted by this role of regional specialist and in some fields (certainly not all) left it to other colleges to make the running when it came to innovation and the intellectual development of the relevant discipline. Since the late 1980s, and especially with the change to direct funding from HEFCE, bypassing Senate House, the University has in many respects ceased to exist. SOAS still proudly awards University of London degrees, but in most other respects its teaches and administers itself pretty much as it likes, subject only to the guidelines and audits that periodically issue from HEFCE. From being part of a vast departmental store, if one can sustain the analogy a little further, SOAS has had to become in some respects more like a well-stocked corner shop that needs to carry everything from Mars bars to broom handles.

There are certainly those at SOAS who regret this transformation and the loss of London-wide collegiality and the remorseless competition and intercollegiate accountancy that it has unleashed. It is alarming when UCL or LSE makes an appointment in a field SOAS conventionally thought of as its own preserve or attracts PhD students who, twenty years ago, would unquestionably have regarded SOAS as their natural home. But, despite some commendable efforts at collaborative ventures (such as the AHRB Centre for Asian and African Literatures operated jointly with UCL), universities and colleges in London as elsewhere find it hard to buck the current trend. The price of finding oneself a corner shop can be high. It has become ever more necessary to create a SOAS Library that is not only a world-class research library but also one that can to a large extent replace the University of London Library as a mainstay of undergraduate and MA student reading, providing coverage of the arts, humanities and social sciences in general and not solely with respect to Asia and Africa. Administratively, too, work that was once done centrally by Senate House has now (with a few exceptions like the administration of PhD examinations) passed to an already heavily burdened SOAS Registry, which under the able leadership of Terry Harvey as Academic Registrar has had to assume a great many regulatory functions previously exercised centrally.

Celebrating independence

But it would be unduly negative – and misleading – to see the virtual demise of the University of London as merely an intolerable increase in the burden placed upon SOAS. In some ways SOAS has been liberated by the new arrangement. It has become possible over the past decade or two for SOAS to think of itself as a university in all but name and to act with a corresponding degree of imagination, autonomy and responsibility. While continuing to capitalize on what the combined reputation and resources of the University of London still provide, the School can feel more confident about maintaining and enhancing its distinctive scholarly identity. It can feel free to provide its undergraduate and Masters students with a better balance than formerly between regional specialization and disciplinary approach, and to pursue research into areas that were once thought to be well beyond the SOAS remit. It has also meant that SOAS can now more freely embark upon collaborative ventures outside the old University arena, with other universities in London and the southeast in particular, as the collaboration with Surrey and Surrey Roehampton in the recently instituted AHRB Centre for Cross-Cultural Music and Dance Performance indicates.

No formal occasion provides a better opportunity for celebrating this independence than the annual Graduation Ceremonies. It is difficult to remember just how recently these replaced the relative anonymity of the University ceremonies which used to include their small delegations of SOAS students. We now have our own quite distinctive rituals: the long lists of international graduands with extraordinarily diverse names that pose such challenges to those who have to read them out, the ever different performances of Asian and African music organized by the Music Department, and the central ceremonial role which was until recently exercised with unflagging wit and patience by Lord Howe as Visitor and which is now performed with equally graceful authority by Baroness Kennedy as President.

Yes, we may reflect at end of each year, SOAS remains in many respects a peculiar institution. In some ways it has the ability to do what almost no other institution in the UK can do – to speak with real academic authority (and even a little passion) about the societies, cultures and polities of two-thirds of the world and indeed about those millions of peoples who have been part of the transnational migrations of the past few centuries and of recent decades. It is an extraordinarily important and privileged position for so small an institution to occupy. And yet at times it seems almost overwhelming. Academics are often all too conscious of the limits of what they know and the multiple interpretations that can be brought to that knowledge, and the study of Asia and Africa have become fields where scholars often speak with far less confidence and clear-cut incisiveness than may have been possible fifty years ago. By comparison with some of the universities against which it measures itself, SOAS has perhaps been too small and too young to speak with full authority. Conversely, it has been too large and diverse to speak with a single voice, and it would be reckless if it did. But in the twenty-first century it can rightly have a more confident sense of its own future and the enormous contribution which it can make to this society and to a world of ever increasing interdependence.

2

A history of SOAS, 1917-67*

Sir Cyril Philips

Beginnings

It was extraordinary that the great age of growth in the British Empire should have been allowed to pass without the formation in London of an imperial training centre. The British response had been to devise a series of *ad hoc* arrangements, including some training for Indian Civil Service probationers at Oxford and Cambridge and at University College, London, and language courses in Hausa and Swahili for Colonial Service officers at King's College. But by the close of the nineteenth century renewed attention had been drawn to the problem of the best way of preparing British officers for imperial administration. Lord Curzon's cult of administrative efficiency in India coincided with a growing awareness in London that existing arrangements were inadequate and that other European countries, with smaller imperial commitments, had gone further in training officials for overseas service and in the scholarly study of the peoples and cultures of Asia.

When, therefore, in 1905 a deputation from the Senate of the University of London sought a meeting with the Prime Minister, Sir Henry Campbell-Bannerman, and his Cabinet colleagues to urge the formation of a School of Oriental Studies as a constituent college within the University, they evoked a favourable response. A departmental committee of inquiry was established with Lord Reay, a former Governor of Bombay, as chairman and Philip Hartog, the University's Academic Registrar, as secretary. Evidence given to the committee was overwhelmingly in favour of the creation of a School of Oriental Studies as part of the University of London. Government departments, commercial organizations, missions and scholars, all agreed that their needs could and should be met in such a School,

---

* Précis by David Arnold from *The School of Oriental and African Studies, University of London, 1917-1967: An Introduction* (SOAS, 1967)

and that its creation was a matter of urgency. In its report in December 1908, the Reay Committee indicated a modest range of studies covering the major languages of the Near East, India, Malaya and Burma, China and Japan and West Africa, which would meet both practical needs and scholarly requirements at an initial recurring cost of £14,000. But it was easy for those with vested interests to say the right things; the acid test was whether they would provide the means to achieve the desired end.

A delay of nine months followed before the Report was published and accepted by Government, and a second committee was formed under Lord Cromer to give practical effect to the Reay Report. Hartog, who had become a passionate convert to the cause of Oriental studies, agreed to carry on as secretary to the new committee and cleared the first, major obstacle by discovering a large building in Finsbury Circus in the City, then occupied by the London Institution, which would be eminently suitable as a home for the School. But it took until the close of 1912 for the transfer to take place and another eighteen months to negotiate a government grant of £25,000 to put the building in order and secure the promise of an annual grant of £4,000. In May 1914 the Committee issued an appeal for an endowment of £100,000, but no sooner had gifts begun to arrive than all operations came to an abrupt halt with the outbreak of the First World War. Nonetheless, on 5 June 1916 the School received its Royal Charter as a College of the University of London and another appeal committee was formed, but the times were out of joint for raising large sums of money and the appeal closed, far short of its target, at £36,267. Hartog appreciated that if any further delays occurred the School might never come into being: in November the Governing Body invited Dr Denison Ross, formerly of the Indian Education Service, to become the first Director and the first students were admitted on 18 January 1917. On 23 February, in the presence of a large gathering, which included Lord Curzon and other members of the War Cabinet, and to the strains of music, both Western and Oriental, the School was formally opened by George V.

Growing pains, 1917-39

The purposes for which the School had been created were stated in the second article of the Royal Charter. As a School of Oriental Studies in the University of London it was 'to give instruction in the Languages of Eastern and African peoples, Ancient and Modern, and in the Literature, History, Religion, and Customs of those peoples, especially with a view to the needs of persons about to proceed to the East or to Africa for the pursuit of study and research, commerce or a profession'. Since in the discussions leading up to the School's foundation the primary emphasis had been on the need to provide practical training for those about to proceed overseas, it was not surprising that initially the Senate of the University of London should give only temporary university recognition to the School for a period of three years and that for the sole purpose of registering students for higher degrees.

With the Director in post and a building ready to start work in, the first task was to recruit staff. Twenty-six of the teachers already concerned with Oriental and African studies at University College and King's College accepted transfer to the School, even though for most no more than part-time employment could be offered. Thus, L. D. Barnett, the Lecturer in Sanskrit, was offered the princely sum of £40 a year and the promise of a share of the fees if his students ever exceeded six in number. On these terms the School ran the risk of not being able to recruit or retain good staff, and the Governors made an urgent appeal for financial help to the Treasury. This only produced the laconic reply from the Financial Secretary that 'the opportunities of earning an income from the teaching of Oriental languages must be so limited that it does not appear to me that you ought to have any difficulty in retaining your existing lecturers or acquiring new ones on existing terms.'

With such restricted resources all that could be attempted in the School's first decade was gradually to transform the part-time into full-time appointments, and to attract, if possible, a nucleus of senior teachers. The University title of Professor of Persian was conferred on the Director, and to this were added by 1922 four further professorships and four readerships. With such names as Thomas Arnold in Arabic, Ralph Turner in Sanskrit, Grahame Bailey in Urdu, Sutton Page in Bengali, and Henry Dodwell in History, the School was assured of a high academic reputation. Initially, teaching was offered in twenty subjects, loosely organized into seven groups, steadily increasing to a total of 74 courses by 1932-33. But the small size of classes, with only two percent attracting eleven or more students, made the School expensive to run and rendered inevitable the use of temporary, hourly-paid labour.

In the aftermath of war, national energies had run low, and the insidious effects of wartime inflation followed by postwar deflation were widely felt. Along with other major national institutions universities suffered, and every part of the School's work in these early years was bedevilled by lack of money. The glaring inadequacies of university salaries in London induced the London County Council to initiate improvements, but although a higher scale was introduced, the School was unable to make the recommended increases. Adamant though he had been in saying that it would be folly to begin with less than £14,000 a year, in fact the first annual estimates presented by Hartog were for an income of £8,806 and an expenditure of £14,065. The budget was eventually balanced, but it was a continuing cause for anxiety that a large proportion of the income was precarious. The only certain elements were the £4,000 annually provided by the Treasury, plus a third of that amount from the London County Council, along with the dividends on the invested appeal money. From the start, too, against all expectations, relatively little use was made of the School by commercial firms. However, an approach to the Treasury made on behalf of all British universities and the emergence of the new university grants system eased the situation, so that the School's Treasury grant rose from £4,000 to £7,000, further increasing in 1921-22 to £12,000 and £13,250 four years later. Even so, annual expenditure regularly exceeded income, and fresh sources of aid had to be sought. In 1925 the Governors authorized the Director to pass round the hat to commercial firms, without success; two years later on the School's tenth anniversary a public appeal for funds was made, again with little response.

For Ross especially, it was a dispiriting period, but he continued to seize every chance of raising money, setting up a committee to formulate applications to charitable trusts, sending begging letters to Indian princes and seeking out likely donors at society dinners. But money was hard to come by, and at the end of it all the School was better off by a mere £750 a year. On the academic side, too, prospects seemed thin. Opinion in the University generally was uneasy at the School's apparent slowness in fulfilling the expectations of the Reay Report, and although recognition for the registration of higher degrees had been renewed periodically, it was agreed that the time had arrived for stocktaking. In particular, attention was directed to the disproportion between the relatively large number of students taking short courses of an elementary and pre-university character and the very small number taking university courses. In 1926-27, for example, only 65 of the 528 students were working for university degrees or School examinations. The only sustained demand for university courses was in history, mainly from students from India.

The Senate accordingly decided to institute a thorough inquiry, meanwhile extending recognition of higher degrees for only one year from March 1927. Against the background of a precarious financial situation, a disappointing response from commerce and industry, and the slow growth of university courses, the School's future as a separate institution seemed to hang in the balance. However, members of the Senate rapidly appreciated the real difficulties with which the School had been grappling and considered that the cost of instruction there 'must always be disproportionate to the income derived from students' fees', and that, until steps had been taken to put the School in a position to meet its annual liabilities, 'each year on the present financial basis involves a lessening of available resources and a nearer approach to ultimate crisis'. Such modest increases of expenditure as had already taken place were deemed unavoidable 'if the School is to fulfil its purpose'. It was recognized, too, that the School had attracted a distinguished professoriate, had achieved through its *Bulletin* an unrivalled reputation for Orientalist scholarship, and that its library was a valuable instrument for future research. These considerations led the Inspectors to conclude that 'the School of Oriental Studies is rendering great services to the State and to the Empire, and in doing so it is reflecting credit upon the University of London, and doing work which the University should be proud to undertake'. In their view its 'continuance on a sound financial basis was not only of University but of Imperial concern'. The Senate fully concurred and extended the School's recognition for both first and higher degrees and in the session that followed approved the introduction of first degree courses in Arabic, Bengali, Chinese, Gujarati, History (with reference to India and to the Near and Middle East), Japanese, Malay, Marathi, Persian, Sanskrit, Pali, Indo-Aryan, Sinhalese, Tamil, Turkish, Urdu and Hindi.

From this scrutiny the School emerged with great credit and, with the prospect of full university status, confidence began to rise. A memorandum urging the need for expansion in both linguistic and cultural studies, including anthropology, was submitted to the University Grants Committee, along with a request for a recurrent increase of £5,000. Syllabuses for the new first degree courses were prepared, even though it was unclear where the students would be found. When it was asked what its attitude would be towards the newly acquired University of London site in Bloomsbury, the School unhesitatingly replied that it would welcome the opportunity of moving to 'the University precinct', coming into closer touch with the central administration and with other colleges and libraries, and thus enabling staff and students to enjoy 'a larger university life'. Following the Senate's vote of confidence, there was also a feeling among some members of the School that its future lay not in providing *ad hoc* training courses but as an advanced centre of university studies.

Thus far, the School's academic and administrative structure had remained relatively unchanged. In theory the final word on academic policy rested with the Academic Board, but this body was too large and miscellaneous in composition to provide effective discussion and leadership, and so in practice control of administrative and academic affairs remained largely in the hands of the Director. Genial, bursting with energy, enthusiasm and good living, and a great conversationalist, Ross carried his responsibilities lightly and never failed to radiate confidence. But, lacking the necessary funds, he found it impossible to look far ahead. On occasion he consulted his senior colleagues, but the system was casual, and, with the University's acceptance of a wide range of new degree courses and the urgent need to raise funds, it became evident that the loose administrative and academic arrangements of the past would have to be replaced. In 1932, therefore, it was decided to reorganize teaching and research into eight departments, six devoted to the study of languages and cultures alongside two others for Oriental history and law and for phonetics and linguistics (the latter marking the formal introduction of a new discipline into British university studies). The six 'regional' departments covered Ancient India and Iran, Modern India and Ceylon, South East Asia and the Islands, the Far East, the Near East and Africa (in 1936 this was reduced to four by absorbing Ancient India and Iran and South East Asia into the other departments). To take charge of each of these a Head of Department was appointed, and all of the Heads were brought together in a committee under the chairmanship of the Director with responsibility for initiating and guiding academic policy. It was a sensible arrangement and one which subsequently served the School well.

For the first time systematic academic planning across the whole range of the School's work became possible, and one of the earliest consequences of this was a proposal for research into linguistics and African languages. Previously, African language teaching had been in the hands of Alice and Mary Werner, and on their retirement an ambitious scheme was propounded by the young phonetician Arthur Lloyd James for the establishment of an international centre of linguistic study, research and teaching, giving special emphasis to spoken African languages. An approach was made to the Rockefeller Foundation for financial support and, through the advice of James Gunn of the Foundation, the rather diffuse original proposal emerged as a compact programme of African linguistic research with an annual budget of £3,000. Through this work, continued with Rockefeller support down to 1938, a nucleus of staff was created under the gifted phonetician, Ida Ward, the Department of Africa was brought into being, and a unique scheme of research and teaching was begun. It was a natural corollary, first suggested in 1935 by Lord Lugard, one of the Governors, that the title of the School should be enlarged to include Africa, which was done three years later.

In this period the pattern of teaching had gradually assumed a new shape, with a growing emphasis on university courses. The pattern and content of university education had been little affected by the growth of the British Empire in Asia and Africa, and apart from government departments seeking training for civil servants, there was little demand by British students for what the School could offer. To most Asian and African studies appeared exotic, even mysterious, and no one concerned with extra-European studies who did not grow up in Britain between the two wars can readily appreciate how restricted were the opportunities then available for British students. The almost total absence of scholarships, travel funds and careers opportunities deterred all but a tiny handful of dedicated young scholars. Although British students taking such courses were few and far between, the traditional attraction of Britain for the dependent countries of the Empire, combined with the presence of a small group of really outstanding scholars (such as Harold Bailey, Hamilton Gibb and Walter Henning), began to draw students from abroad, especially for postgraduate study. It was ironic that it should have been university students from overseas rather than from Britain who for many years benefited most from SOAS. By 1927-28 the School had 115 overseas students, rising by 1936-37 to 174, nearly 40 percent of the student population of 428. Despite this increase in work of university standard, the bulk of the teaching was still in the form of short courses, usually of several months' duration and mainly on behalf of Government, business firms and missions. The demand from firms for this type of course constituted less than fifteen percent of the whole, and a renewed attempt to redress this imbalance was made by offering Commercial Certificates to those completing the short course, but demand fell and the scheme was abandoned. Conversely, the longer, more testing first – and second – year School Certificates and Diplomas, mainly in language studies, served a small but steady demand and were maintained. The School had begun to turn away from providing short courses of a sub-university character towards the development of university courses, but progress was slow.

Consistent with this trend, when the University offered SOAS space within the Bloomsbury precinct it was accepted with alacrity. The Finsbury building was sold in July 1935 for £219,000, and pending erection of a new building in Bloomsbury temporary premises were rented in Westminster while the library moved to Clarence House, near St James's Park. The Finsbury building had served its purpose admirably, and no one who worked there is likely to forget either its cellars, which for long provided the common rooms for staff and students, or its serene and lovely library reading room, whose wooden floors and panelling glowed with subdued light. Had the School been able to foresee that, through the vicissitudes of war and peace, it was to be denied for more than thirty years the facility of a new library building, it might well have hesitated to make the move. But the decision to move from the City to Bloomsbury formed a critical turning-point in the School's history. Remoteness had encouraged academic isolation: the School was in the University but not of it. As Henry Dodwell pointed out, it was of immense benefit for a small, young college, in which there were few long-established traditions, to move into the heart of the University; symbolically it was right, too, that Asian and African studies should take a central place in the world exchange developing in our own time.

Plans for the new building, which was to accommodate an academic staff of forty, a library of several hundred thousand volumes, a small administrative staff and an undeclared number of students, were quickly prepared and approved. So smoothly beguiling was this progress that the Governors could be forgiven for optimistically announcing in 1938 that 'the School would be installed in its Bloomsbury home by March 1941'. Time and again in the matter of new buildings hope triumphed over experience. Since the sale of the Finsbury building apparently met the School's capital needs, renewed emphasis accordingly fell on the inadequacy of the recurrent funds. Annual income had crept up to £20,000 by the early 1920s and to £30,000 through the following decade. Renewed appeals to the City elicited no response, and it became obvious that industry and commerce were so preoccupied with the economic slump that the School's only hope lay in trying on national grounds to obtain greater Government support. The gathering political tension between the European powers and German, Italian and Japanese ambitions in Asia and Africa encouraged this switch of emphasis. With some Departments of State the School's association was close. From the start the India Office had recognized the value of its work in training Indian Civil Service probationers by making an annual grant of £1,250 (later rising to £2,250), but no similar recurring grant (except for £30 from Hong Kong) had ever been made by the Colonial Office or by colonial governments. A carefully coordinated approach made to all of the colonial governments evoked £4,380 for the 1938-39 session, and the Treasury grant was raised to £17,433. By this period, therefore, annual income and expenditure had reached nearly £40,000, but, with one-third of income still drawn from *ad hoc* annual grants and donations, the School's programme of work was far from secure, the rate of growth of staff was small and long-term planning impossible.

The reading room at Finsbury Circus

At this juncture Ross retired and was succeeded in 1938 by Ralph Turner, who had first joined the School in 1922 as Professor of Sanskrit, after serving in the Indian Education Service and in Allenby's army in Palestine. Ross had managed against heavy odds to keep the School alive. This was a considerable achievement, but he had not been able to make it the imperial and practical training centre envisaged by the Reay Report, or to define clearly the School's function as a college of the University. It may be that the two functions were not easily reconcilable. The move to Bloomsbury was to prove decisive, but time had to elapse before this could be appreciated. Meanwhile, other urgent considerations had to be faced. Taking over in a period of national emergency, Turner naturally saw his primary task as preparing the School to meet any demands which British involvement in a major war in Asia and Africa would impose on it. News continued to reach London of the great strides in Asian and African studies being taken by Germany and Italy, and this threw into high relief the scantiness of the School's resources, the fragility of its academic structure, and the lack of a British national policy. A case for putting the situation right, especially building up the coverage of strategically important languages, was hurriedly prepared and submitted to the Secretaries of State for India and the Colonies and to the Financial Secretary of the War Office. An inter-departmental committee was established to assess the cost of the School's urgent needs, which were put at £25,000 a year. Hopes ran high, but the Treasury rejected the committee's recommendation on the ground of economy.

Meanwhile, assuming that in the event of war London would be bombed, arrange-ments were made to evacuate the School to Cambridge, where accommodation was found at Christ's College. When war broke out in September 1939, the School found itself in temporary quarters, its financial resources fully committed to a half-completed building in Bloomsbury, its staff scattered, its library in storage and with the bitter knowledge that its teaching establishment was still deficient in every department. Founded in the closing stages of the First World War to meet national needs, financially half-starved in the two decades of peace, it nervously braced itself to respond to a challenge of a totally new order.

The war years, 1939-46

It was only with the greatest hesitation and on Government's advice that the School left London for Cambridge, and as soon as it became clear that, despite the air raids, it was possible to resume work there, a return was made in July 1940. There had never been any question but that in time of war the School's proper place was to be in close touch with the Service Ministries and Departments of State. The half-completed building in Bloomsbury received a direct hit in September 1940, but repairs were at once made and construction continued. Anticipating an early entry into its new home, the School found temporary quarters in Broadway Court, overlooking St James's station, and was dismayed to learn that the Ministry of Information, already installed in Senate House, wanted to occupy the whole of the new building as well. Battle was joined for possession, Sir Philip Hartog, now a Governor and as dedicated and selfless as ever, energetically leading what proved to be his last fight on behalf of the School. But it was not until February 1943 that a solution was found whereby the shell of the whole building as originally planned was to be completed, the School occupying the two upper floors and part of the basement, and the Ministry the remainder on condition that it would vacate six months after the war's end.

It had been assumed in 1917 that the School would have a significant part to play in any future world conflict, but by 1939, despite the long, preceding period of international tension, only the most tentative indication had been given by the War Office that in the event of war it foresaw the need for some courses in Arabic, Persian, Turkish, Japanese and Siamese. But no steps had been taken to put the School in funds or ensure that teachers would be available, and by late 1941 only two of these courses had been firmly requested. Some work had voluntarily been contributed, including research by the Phonetics Section into radio-telephone speech for the Air Ministry, and a short course for officials of the Colonial Office and British Council. But this constituted a ludicrously small contribution to the war effort, and the Director found it alarming that, despite the increasing scale of conflict in the Middle East and Africa and the threat of war in the Far East, no far-reaching programme of language training for the Services was even being considered. When SOAS volunteered to give a short course in Urdu for officers and cadets for the Indian Army, the cost of the fees being met by the War Office, 365 servicemen took up the offer.

In mid-1941 the School made formal representations to the Foreign Office and War Office, pointing to the critical British shortage of experts in Japanese and to the long period of training needed to acquire a knowledge of that language. However, the War Office response, in August 1941, was discouraging. 'So far as can be reasonably foreseen at present', it said, 'we feel we are ... reasonably insured in the matter of officers knowing Oriental languages.' Two months later Britain was at war with Japan and the Intelligence Departments were desperately casting around for men able to read and speak Japanese. When the School renewed the offer its services were accepted, but eight months were still to elapse before any servicemen actually arrived for instruction. Once trained, they were eagerly snapped up, and so great was the military need in the Indian and Far Eastern fields of war that those whose only training was a ten weeks' course in recognizing and recording Japanese radio signals, were on arrival in India pressed into translating documents. After this slow start, the basic courses were built up steadily, and by October 1945 nearly 600 men had qualified. Large numbers of radio-telephonists with some knowledge of Japanese were required, but the preparation of a short, effective course offered peculiar difficulties. Lloyd James, Head of the Department of Phonetics and Linguistics, made some initial explorations of the problem, cut short by his tragic illness and death, but his successor, the energetic and ingenious J. R. Firth, devised a system by which men could be trained in a very short period to record accurately. The Royal Air Force sent its first men for this course in October 1942, and assuming that the Fleet Air Arm would have like needs, the School gave a similar invitation to the Admiralty, which showed no immediate interest. Within a year, however, the Navy was vainly trying to borrow trained men from the RAF and by August 1943 was sending its own men to SOAS for training. As the war in the East unfolded, it became obvious that links with China would be of great importance, and the Director approached the War Office on the likely need for men trained in Chinese. He got little encouragement, the War Office responding that 'educated Chinese spoke English' and so liaison officers 'had no need to speak Chinese'. As previously with Japanese, the advice rejected in 1942 was taken in 1945, by which time the Services had sent 71 men for Chinese training.

As the demands of war mounted, SOAS was called on to undertake a wider range of work. The Postal and Telegraph Censorship Department enlisted its aid in reading letters in languages which could not be dealt with in the Uncommon Languages Section. More than 32,000 letters in 192 languages were dealt with in this way during the war, reaching a peak of over one thousand a month in early 1945. The demand for intensive language courses continued to grow, bringing into the School, for example, in 1943-44 about a thousand servicemen, and in the process over-whelming the School's accommodation and necessitating the transfer of the Far Eastern courses to some converted houses in Sussex Gardens. Altogether 1,674 servicemen passed through courses at SOAS between 1942 and 1946. With the accompanying rise in fee income, the School's financial troubles seemed to be over, and modest annual surpluses accrued. But this buoyancy was more apparent than real, the annual grant from the University being still only £21,000, and it seemed certain that the School's financial position would be no more secure in the postwar period than it had been previously. Thought in Britain was everywhere turning to the postwar world, creating a climate of opinion favourable to development and change. It was to be expected that in the context of its assumed national role, SOAS should wish to re-examine its own position and the inadequacy of the provision for those studies for which it carried a major responsibility. The war, especially the initial debacle in the Far East and the associated failure of British military intelligence, could not but provoke renewed discussion on national needs, both practical and academic. In many respects the School still fell short of what the Reay Report had proposed, and the sharp comparison of reality with what appeared urgently necessary to sustain the war effort evoked from departments a succession of plans for development, first for Near and Far Eastern studies, then for Indian studies, and in February 1944 the Foreign Office requested another consolidated statement of need. A comprehensive summary of these proposals was gathered together and presented as a plan for expansion over a ten-year period from the end of the war. The School founded its case less on wartime military needs than on the likelihood of great changes in postwar Asia and Africa. 'The tide of nationalism', it said, 'is running high in every Oriental and African country, and the peoples of those countries look forward to great economic development, industrial, commercial and agricultural. In this they will welcome the assistance of the West, but not in the bygone spirit of submission to Western authority.' An expansion of Oriental and African studies in British universities would assist in preparing and equipping Britain to take a full and sympathetic part in these changes, and in adjusting her outlook and policies accordingly. SOAS estimated that it would need for these purposes a recurrent grant of £35,000, rising to £125,000 by the end of the decade, along with a £100,000 capital grant to enlarge its accommodation.

In interviews with the Minister for War and the Secretary of State for India, the Director argued that the time was ripe for a Government commission to review the future of Oriental and African studies in Britain, and Lord Hailey, then Chairman of the School's Governors, added his powerful voice. The movement of world affairs, the ebb and flow of British fortunes, favoured the proposal, and the great changes brought about by the war in Asia and Africa, and the wartime alliance with Russia had made it urgently necessary to make a fresh appraisal of Britain's position. In June 1944 Anthony Eden, Secretary of State for Foreign Affairs, announced the Government's intention of setting up a commission 'to examine the facilities offered by universities and other educational institutions in Britain for the study of Oriental, Slavonic, East European, and African languages and cultures, to consider what advantage is being taken of these facilities and to formulate recommendations for their improvement'. The Commission began its inquiries in 1945 under the chairmanship of Lord Scarbrough. A former Governor of Bombay and Minister for India and Burma, no one was more eminently fitted for the task.

The Scarbrough Report, completed in April 1946 and published the following year, formed a milestone in the development of these studies in Britain. It declared that the war had given a clear indication of the importance which increasing contacts between countries would assume subsequently and of the growing significance of Asia, Africa and the Slavonic world. It had also revealed Britain's deficiencies in the number of persons available to provide expert knowledge and teaching about their governments and peoples. In the Commission's opinion, this kind of knowledge in a world at peace, no less than one at war, had to find a permanent and growing place in British culture, starting in the universities, where the existing scale of research and teaching was quite inadequate to meet Britain's needs. The first requirement was to build strong university departments, primarily in the study of languages, with some related cultural studies, in place of a few isolated professorial posts in several British universities. As a means to recruit staff for these new departments, Treasury studentships were proposed, and provision was also to be made for those so trained to keep up-to-date by travel abroad. The Commission was not deterred by the expectation that for some time to come the number of undergraduates would be small, declaring that the national importance of these studies and the evident need for much more research justified exceptional treatment. In this proposed programme of growth it recognized that all of the fields of study relating to Asia and Africa would be developed in the University of London, mainly at SOAS, and that for economy, convenience and efficiency the study of the languages of Africa and South East Asia in particular should be concentrated there. Incisive in its analysis and practical in its recommendations, the Report received a warm and enthusiastic welcome.

The fulfilment of the Report was expected to require a period of ten years, the likely annual cost at the halfway stage being £225,000, with a similar increase over a second five-year period. The Government accepted these recommendations and allocated the recurrent sums required as an earmarked grant for the first five years, and the University Grants Committee invited selected universities to submit proposals for development. The School submitted the scheme of expansion it had previously drawn up, being prompted by the Commission's chairman to raise its sights and increase the scale of its proposals.

Expansion and recovery, 1946-57

Well in advance of any money forthcoming under the Scarbrough proposals, the School had been promised by the University of London that its recurrent grant would be raised to £60,000 annually for the 1947-52 quinquennium. At the same time Government's adoption of the Devonshire Report on Colonial Service training had assured the School of a grant for African language studies, so for the first time SOAS knew that it could rely on an ample surplus, could start on its postwar programme, and take a long view of future development. A ten-year period of expansion was envisaged in which the academic establishment of 63 posts would rise by the halfway stage to 218 posts and at the close in 1957 to 256 posts, providing for general growth in the humanities, with emphasis on the study of history, language and literature and a modest addition in law and anthropology.

Following decades of financial stringency, academic frustration and wartime disturbance, this was a formidable and far-reaching programme, but one in keeping with the times. A new Labour Government, pledged to a policy of reform and development, had taken office, the unexpectedly quick victory in the Far East had uplifted the national spirit, and the minds of people everywhere were set on fulfilling ambitious plans formulated to keep hope alive in the dark days of war. There was no reason why those who had long called for the expansion of the School should question the correctness of this policy or the School's ability to carry through such a massive enterprise. However, before the war SOAS had been fortunate in getting teachers of distinction from the missionary societies and overseas services, not least in India. With the winding down of these services it was obvious that everything depended on the School's ability to attract young British scholars into these new fields of study. A score of temporary teachers, especially in Chinese and Japanese, had been recruited from servicemen to run wartime courses, and there were large numbers of demobilized servicemen about to return from Asia and Africa, many of whom it was assumed would have an enduring interest in those areas. From these sources alone SOAS thought it could fill as many as one hundred Scarbrough training scholarships.

Bearing in mind the Commission's advice on building strong departments, the School proposed expanding the existing four nuclei formed by the teachers of the principal languages and literatures of Asia and Africa, whose work had long been organized on a regional basis, as well as the small but long-established units of phonetics and linguistics and of history and law. All six departments set to with a will to recruit and train staff, but some made quicker progress than others. Under the stimulating sway of J. R. Firth, the Department of Phonetics and Linguistics expanded in numbers and maintained its leadership role in these fields. In History, the whole of the quinquennial quota of twenty new posts was completed, covering all of the major Asian areas in ancient and modern times, and a start was made in the pre-European history of Africa. Attracting students from throughout the world, especially from South Asia, the History Department grew within a decade into the largest research department in a British university. In the regional departments the principal increases were made by India, Pakistan and Ceylon (with 29 established posts), by the Near and Middle East (26) and the Far East (26), with roughly half on the language side, chiefly on the modern spoken tongues, and half in philosophy, religion, the history of art and archaeology. The Africa Department reached an establishment of twenty posts in language studies, but progress in the South East Asia field was slow, for the Department, dissolved in 1936, had first to be recreated under J. A. Stewart.

On the advice of the University Grants Committee (UGC) the small number of teachers in law and anthropology, hitherto attached to other departments, were grouped together to form Departments of Law (1947) and Anthropology (1949), under Seymour Vesey-Fitzgerald and Christoph von Fürer-Haimendorf respectively, but not without reservation from some in the regional departments who feared that process of sub-division might be carried to extremes and who preferred to keep all the disciplines within the regional departments. But this would have produced overlarge and administratively cumbrous departments, cutting across the established lines of development elsewhere in the University. Desirable though in some ways it may have been to promote regional or 'area studies', the regional departments had not yet turned their attention to this problem of organizing area studies within the existing framework of teaching either at the undergraduate or postgraduate stages. Moreover, the creation of new departments by discipline, on the same lines as History or Phonetics and Linguistics, not only facilitated their rapid growth, but also ensured the maintenance of high standards by establishing them as integral members of the relevant University boards in these studies. These were crucial decisions, for once taken it became virtually impossible, even if desirable, to accept 'area studies' as the sole conceptual framework within which to foster the School's work.

Despite high hopes and great endeavours, many of the quinquennial objectives were not achieved. It proved impossible to award more than 24 Treasury studentships, and by the close of the period the net increase in academic staff was only about one hundred. But SOAS remained confident that the entire Scarbrough programme could be fulfilled and looked forward in the 1952-57 period to adding a further 29 posts. No new major departments were envisaged and the aim was to consolidate existing studies in the humanities, along with modest growth in law and anthropology. However, the start of the second quinquennium in 1952 coincided with one of Britain's recurring postwar financial crises and universities immediately felt the cold wind of economy. With increased competition for funds within each university, Oriental departments with small undergraduate numbers were ill placed to assert their priority. Hitherto they had been protected by the earmarking of their grants, but this policy was generally suspect in the universities and the Scarbrough Commission itself had taken the view that it did 'not think it necessary or even desirable that this arrangement should be a permanent one'. The UGC decided to discontinue the earmarked grants for the new quinquennium and, 'in the best interests of the Oriental and African departments', leave them to compete for funds with other University departments. With such a poor competitive position, especially relative to the sciences, Oriental departments fared very badly, and in most universities their growth came to an abrupt halt. As a grant-receiving college, SOAS continued to enjoy steadfast support from the University Court and so suffered less than most. But all London colleges suffered cuts and the School's recurrent grant, of between £15,000 and £50,000 in the first quinquennium, fell in the second to, on average, £8,000. However, it was still possible to maintain some momentum, and in the following five years 26 new posts were added, representing one-eighth of the proposed programme.

Although unable to fulfil the Scarbrough targets, in 1955, as plans were prepared for the following quinquennium, the School reaffirmed its intention of completing the original proposals by adding a further 53 posts. By this stage the regional departments had reached a considerable size, India, Pakistan and Ceylon comprising 26 posts, the Near and Middle East 31, the Far East 28 and Africa 21, so that a reasonable scale of teaching was possible for all the major and many minor languages. But one adverse consequence of the preoccupation with staff expansion was inadequate attention to the general failure of Oriental departments to attract British students, despite the overall rise in student numbers. The number of undergraduates at SOAS actually fell from 62 in 1952-53 to 56 in 1956-57, so that the question was bound sooner or later to be asked how far the Scarbrough policy of building strong departments, independent of undergraduate demand, was to be taken, and in particular how far young scholars were to be recruited and trained for posts which would inevitably be largely devoted to research. It had been assumed that student numbers at SOAS would decline from the very large figure at the end of the war with the termination of courses for servicemen and the running down of training courses for the Indian Civil Service and the Colonial Office. Some decline, too, was expected as the bigger firms instituted their own training schemes. There was, however, an expectation that some growth in student numbers would follow from the large increases in staff. Yet in 1956-57, ten years after the Scarbrough Report, there was no sign of an increasing undergraduate demand in Oriental and African Studies, and the failure to attract British students appeared likely to undermine the future of these studies in the United Kingdom. The number of British undergraduates at SOAS had fallen from 55 in 1947-48 to 27 in 1952-53 and 22 in 1956-57: in 1960-61 there were only 20 British students out of 217. To make matters worse, a Treasury decision to economize by restricting Scarbrough studentships to persons already assured of appointment to a university post effectively cut back the programme and the studentship scheme slowly withered away.

These trends, evident in all Oriental departments in British universities, raised questions of great importance for the future of Asian and African studies and of SOAS, but they were not susceptible to easy answers and thorough consideration of them had unfortunately been deferred and overshadowed by the pressing problem of how to accommodate the enlarged number of staff and growing library collections. The School's buildings as originally planned in the mid-1930s were meant to provide for a staff about a third of that actually reached by 1957 and a library collection of about a quarter, and of those buildings, one wing and a fourth floor remained unbuilt, while the east wing was still only a shell with temporary partitions. The library was reduced to such expedients as reducing to a minimum the width of gangways and raising the height of stacks, and storing books in scattered and often unsuitable store-rooms, including off-site. Five houses in Woburn Square and some rooms in Tavistock Square, made available by the University, provided sub-standard space for fifty to sixty members of staff, but there was a complete lack of large classrooms and purpose-built accommodation. Even the assembly hall was used as a library reading room and the small and unsuitable provision for students was lamentable. Enlarged accommodation had become the overriding need of the School. The University agreed to allocate a site for development adjacent to the School, but low priority was given to capital funds for building purposes.

The 1960s: Growth and transformation

In 1957 Sir Ralph Turner retired from the directorship, being succeeded by Cyril Philips, Head of the Department of History since 1947. In Turner's twenty years as Director, SOAS had been transformed and given a heightened sense of national purpose. The Scarbrough programme had not been completed, but two-thirds of the intended staff increase had been achieved. A substantial number of young British scholars had been attracted to Asian and African studies, strong departments had been created and a sound foundation of scholarship had been laid, particularly in the study of languages and history. But important questions of policy could no longer be deferred. It was already plain that the quinquennium grant for 1957-62, which yielded an annual recurrent increase of £9,000, would not enable the School to complete the Scarbrough programme. There was some realization, too, that, given the failure to attract undergraduates, it would be a mistake to increase academic posts which could have little relevance to under-graduates. The time had arrived to broaden the School's range of teaching, and particularly to emphasize its interest in the study of modern and contemporary Asian and African societies, by further expanding its commitment to history, law and anthropology and by including economics, politics, sociology and geography.

However, building up the social sciences depended on a host of uncertainties, including whether money for the purpose could be raised from the UGC or elsewhere. Nothing could be attempted without additional funds and it was the willingness of the Ford, Leverhulme, Nuffield and Rockefeller Foundations to support new academic enterprise at SOAS which tipped the balance and enabled SOAS to embark on the long and costly operation of training economists, economic historians, sociologists, political scientists, geographers and lawyers equipped with a knowledge not only of their own disciplines but also of the languages, history and culture of Asia and Africa, and reinforced by first-hand experience in the field. This was a difficult pioneering effort because no such development on this scale for Asia and Africa had been attempted previously in the United Kingdom. Success, if achieved, would in the long run not only enhance the scholarly and practical contribution of the School but also exert a revolutionary influence upon British studies in these fields.

Meanwhile the basic question of how to attract students, especially undergraduates, had come under close scrutiny. In History, where a rich choice of courses was already offered, combining the study of Europe with that of Asia or Africa, the position was academically satisfactory, attractive to would-be students and capable of sustained development. But the majority of honours degree courses at the School were in the study of Asian and African languages and literatures, many of which were never likely to be in steady demand. Courses for first degrees in Arabic, Chinese and Japanese attracted substantial numbers but were in need of review. Their suitability as three-year courses of study, for British students in particular, who had to begin from scratch, had to be reconsidered. The educational case for a four-year undergraduate course was very strong and gradually this change was brought about in the majority of language courses. Some teachers were convinced that a good, general education for undergraduates could best be provided through a twin-subject syllabus, combining the study of a language with equal emphasis on a related discipline, or by combining two disciplines with a regional focus. An experiment of this kind, including study in both language and anthropology with special reference to Africa, was started in 1955, but few students had been attracted and other regional departments were cautious about extending this kind of course to Asia.

While some of the existing syllabuses were being revised and made more attractive to British students, the related question of how to make direct contact with prospective students and enlarge the catchment area in Britain was examined. It was essential for the School not only to devise appropriate university courses but also to create direct contact with schools. Such a programme could best be achieved through an extramural division making personal contact with head teachers and their staffs. An education officer, supported by a committee, including representatives of the Ministry of Education and Science and the Ministry of Overseas Development, was appointed for this purpose. Meetings between schools and small teams from SOAS were held, a regular programme of lectures and one-day courses for teachers and sixth-formers was devised with the aid of the Leverhulme Trust, and a scheme of schoolteacher fellowships was instituted. Assisted by the national rise in demand for university places, the declining trend in the undergraduate intake was reversed, and the number of British undergraduates rose from 31 in 1957-18 to 137 (out of 199) in 1961-62. Thereafter the undergraduate intake remained at roughly this level, which was as much as the School's restricted accommodation would allow.

These new policy directions received a powerful impetus from a report published in 1961 by a committee of the UGC set up under the chairmanship of Sir William Hayter to review progress made since the Scarbrough Report and to advise on future developments. The Hayter Report concluded that the overriding need was not so much the completion of the Scarbrough expansion as the reinforcement of the study of the modern societies of Asia and Africa, especially in the social sciences. This should be done, it said, with earmarked grants over a ten-year period. Government accepted the Hayter programme and the UGC established a special sub-committee to supervise the allocation of earmarked funds in the first five years (1962-67), to provide a pool of lectureships and concentrate effort in six university centres of Asian and three of African studies, including SOAS. These proposals, which assured the School a modest allocation of ten lectureships, came with just enough support to enable the social scientists already in training under

Foundation funds to be absorbed into the permanent staff, and to facilitate the creation of a Department of Economic and Political Studies under Edith Penrose, a new sociology section under Ronald Dore and a new Department of Geography under Charles Fisher, besides permitting the strengthening of the regional departments, Anthropology, History and Law. With these additions, the School's broad framework of studies in the humanities and social sciences was erected and given a new orientation.

In the changed climate brought about in British universities by the publication of the Robbins Report in 1963, earlier hesitations at the School about the desirability of introducing undergraduate courses in combined and area studies were swept away, and additional degree courses in history and language, and in languages and anthropology with reference to Asia and Africa, were launched. Simultaneously, the introduction by the University of a one-year Masters course provided the opportunity for a comprehensive postgraduate programme of combined studies for each of the major extra-European areas, including those covered by SOAS. A new source of recruitment had thus been uncovered. Within the School the introduction of postgraduate courses of this scale and complexity precipitated the long-discussed formation of five Area Centres for African, Near and Middle Eastern, South Asian, South East Asian and Far Eastern studies, through which both postgraduate teaching and interdisciplinary studies and research could be fostered and extended. The Area Centres, which included all members of staff of the relevant area of study, were intended to reinforce and complement, not to replace, the departmental system, to create an organic scheme of area study, and encourage the initiation of programmes of work of national and international relevance. By the start of 1966-67 the School was thus in a position to offer a comprehensive range of courses to students from Britain and overseas and to enlarge its already formidable scale of research.

With 200 academic staff, an enlarged student body and a fast-growing library, attention returned to the vexed problem of accommodation. The Hayter Committee had been shocked by SOAS's lack of amenities and yet, with no assistance forthcoming from Government or the University, it was plain the School would have to help itself. Funds were scraped together from the sale of the Finsbury building and accumulated surpluses to extend accommodation in Tavistock Square and to add a fourth floor to the main building, thus providing space for classrooms and staff. For the new library a private appeal was directed by Sir Neville Gass, the Treasurer, a man of vision, charm and unsparing endeavour. Nearly a quarter of a million pounds was raised which enabled the School to take up a characteristically generous offer from the Rockefeller Foundation. Plans for the new building were put in hand under the architect Denys Lasdun, though it was apparent that the costs would be high, probably well over £1.5 million.

From the outset the School had allocated a good proportion of its income to building up its library, by the mid-1960s a major national and international resource, with some 290,000 volumes, and to making its collections available to all serious students in the United Kingdom. As a result of this and the central role the School could play within the British educational system as a whole, the Hayter Committee put forward (and the UGC accepted) the proposal that the SOAS Library should be given the financial support 'to operate fully as a national library'. From this decision two lines of policy stemmed, firstly that the School should initiate close co-operation between interested university libraries, including those associated with the newly established Asian and African centres, and secondly that SOAS should prepare a union catalogue of all works on Asia and ascertain the cost of acquiring all new and significant publications relating to Asia and Africa. This was found in 1965 to be £35,000 a year, and with UGC help SOAS set itself to reach this scale of book collection, which meant doubling its existing outlay, and to increase its staff of specialized librarians. Agreements between relevant libraries were reached, providing for a division of responsibility in acquiring materials relating to African countries. A start was made in the same direction for India, also in exploring the possibility of co-operation among librarians in making field visits for book purchases, and in book selection and cataloguing.

During this period, too, co-operative and interdisciplinary staff research regularly found expression in international conferences. Meetings on 'Historical Writing on the Peoples of Asia' (1956 and 1958), 'African History and Archaeology' (1953, 1957, 1961), and on 'Linguistic Comparison in South East Asia and the Pacific' (1961 and 1965) not only produced important advances in knowledge but also created a foundation and framework of reference for the future. Advanced study groups, for example on agricultural reform in China, revolution in Asia and Africa, the Partition of India, or the economic history of the Middle East, became a normal part of SOAS activity. One mark of the School's standing was the readiness of the great foundations to contribute to its research funds, and in these years Ford, Leverhulme, Nuffield, Gulbenkian, Rockefeller and Wenner Gren between them gave grants amounting to many hundreds of thousands of pounds. The School's contribution to research was remarkable. Its *Bulletin*, long accepted as one of the leading journals of Orientalist scholarship, did much to maintain its international reputation, and from the School and its academic staff there flowed an impressive and varied stream of publications. These included new journals, such as the *Journal of African History*, the *Journal of African Law*, the *Journal of Development Studies* and in 1966-67, in co-operation with the new Asian centres at Cambridge, Hull, Leeds and Sheffield, *Modern Asian Studies*. Through its Publications Committee, the School supported the publication of academic monograph series, including an Oriental Series, an African Language Series and Studies on Modern Asia and Africa.

With its considerable size and comprehensive spread of studies, with its ready access to London's unrivalled resources, with its record of achievement and tradition of fine scholarship, and established capacity for leadership, the School had by the mid-1960s shown a unique potential for growth. It possessed the power and experience, along with the duty and privilege, to maintain itself nationally and internationally as a centre of excellence, and thus to make a nobler, richer and more profound contribution to the welfare of mankind. But one lesson for the School, perhaps the outstanding lesson of the first fifty years of its history, was that institutions, like men, must make their opportunities, as oft as find them.

3

Directors and directions

Richard Rathbone

The Directors' role

In the ninety years or so since its foundation, SOAS has been unusual in having been led and governed by an extremely limited number of what we would now call 'senior managers'. Sir Cyril Philips retired as Director sixty years after the foundation of the School and did so as only its third Director. In the nearly thirty years which have followed Sir Cyril's distinguished tenure, four Directors (or, more correctly, three Directors and one Director and Principal) have held the post; but with the exception of the two most recent Directors, the second of whom took over only in May 2001, Philips's successors have held office for notably long periods. Irrespective, then, of the individual characters and capacities of each of these men, these structural features have ensured that the history of the School has been shaped in large measure by a very small number of personalities. As this has been further underlined by the particularities of the School's Charter, and its procedures both formal and informal, which have given Directors considerable but not absolute powers, there is a tendency to see the history of SOAS as one might see the unfolding history of a monarchy, a sequence of periods each of whose individuality is intimately connected and then identified with the particular personality and capacities of individual kings or queens.

Such a view obviously distorts reality. Although they might have wished otherwise, successive Directors have not been free agents. Each of them has been forced to work within the specific structural and historical constraints over which they have had little control. As the State has been, throughout the School's life, its most significant paymaster, national policies for higher education have very significantly reduced (and have often dictated) the choices open to the School's management. In general terms these policies have progressively reduced the freedom of the School's management as the practical implications of a more and more pervasive culture of accountability and transparency have been imposed upon the public services including higher education. Similarly Directors have not enjoyed an entirely free hand as each of them has had to encourage the support of (and then carry) their Governing Bodies, their Academic Boards and until the 1980s, the Vice-Chancellor and the ruling councils of the University of London. Nor have they acted alone, for Directors have also directed with the significant, if uneven, assistance of formally appointed senior administrators and those senior School officers who have been drawn from the ranks of the teaching staff. These too have constituted a small, but strikingly long-serving, cohort. For over fifty years the post of the School's senior civil servant, the Secretary, has been held by only six men, one of whom served for only two years before his sad, premature death. And while the title has confusingly changed with great frequency, the post of Director's deputy has been filled by a severely limited number of senior scholars.

There are few discernible regularities which are more than mere coincidence in these sorts of data. The vast majority of these actors were both white and male and this regrettable fact is, of course, shared with the histories of vast majority of similar senior posts in British higher education over the same period. There are exceptions to the generalization about gender; an obvious but not the only example lies in the significant post of Librarian , a post which has been held in the recent past by two distinguished women, Barbara Burton and Mary Auckland. Three Directors have been drawn from the field of history. For reasons which are not entirely clear this discipline has also been considerably over-represented in the ranks of Deans and Pro-Directors in the past thirty years in contrast with the notable under-representation of social scientists in those posts.

The Philips era

Sir Cyril Philips's vigorous intellectual imagination and his astute understanding and skilful operation of the shifting politics of higher education in the 1950s and 1960s were in large measure responsible for the great transformation and the modernization of the School during his period in office. SOAS had long been a small, specialist, often eccentric and certainly fragile institution. By the time Philips left the Directorship, the School had a new look of and, even more importantly, a sense of permanence. At long last it had what then felt like a capacious new building, now quite appropriately called the Philips Building, in which to house its library collection as well as office and teaching space. The architect Denys Lasdun's characteristically stark, modernist extension, which at the time some found exciting and others found brutal, was a physical refutation of those who continued to regard the School as a bastion of arcane, disengaged scholarship. Opened quite literally to the sound of natural trumpets in a splendid ceremony which contrasted considerably with Philips's austere personal style, the very structure of the building reflected the Director's own understanding of the nature of scholarship and hence that of the School. The Library lies physically at the heart of that building, just as in his thinking it lay at the heart of the School's endeavours. The world of learning quickly recognized the benefits as the construction of the new building enabled the Librarian to bring together a fine research collection which had previously been scattered in a variety of different depositories.

At the same time the new building allowed the growing number of academics and their students working in the increasing number of departments to share the same space. Colleagues whose working lives had been spent in a number of locations within a wide swathe of temporary lettings in the Bloomsbury area were now far more likely to encounter one another in the corridor, at lunch, in the Senior Common Room. While this in-gathering was to prove to be only a temporary pleasure – the School's continuing expansion ensured that within a very few years whole departments would once again be forced into exile – it served another of the major changes which Philips had initiated. At the heart of his enthusiastic support for the idea of Area Studies Centres lay his belief in interdisciplinarity; and this in turn was facilitated by the fact that teachers from all the School's departments now worked on one site and shared an airy, if smoky, Senior Common Room. The consolidation of the Library also worked to support the vivid increase in undergraduate numbers just as it lay behind the success of the Masters programmes which were launched from the mid-1960s.

Philips's impact was to be felt not only in the development of teaching and research and, of course, bricks and mortar – or rather Lasdun's pre-stressed concrete. In many respects Philips set the style of the institution. Working entirely within the Charter and the School's rules, Philips dominated the governance of the School. Working in close concert with two very formal, very proper and somewhat intimidating School Secretaries, H. Moyse-Bartlett and John Bracken, Philips chaired Academic Board amiably but always firmly. While he did not exercise this control without challenge – many meetings were enlivened by vivid, if always polite, exchanges between the left-wing scholar Ralph Russell and the Director –

Philips's wishes were only very rarely resisted. The Board was dominated by professors who enjoyed membership simply because they were professors; and many of them were Heads of Department who could and often would exercise this authority and its attendant patronage until retirement. The elected element of Academic Board constituted a numerical minority and while the eventual addition of the Chairmen of the Centres of Area Studies might have brought down the average age of the Board, it cannot be claimed that it transformed it, let alone radicalized it. Speaking-up in front of this somewhat baronial gathering when that same group were also those who controlled one's chances of tenure and promotion required courage, or even recklessness, not least because of the fear of disturbing meetings whose highpoint for many was the discreet distribution of tea and biscuits by hushed members of the catering staff. At the same time as Philips was a mostly constructive leader, the hierarchical quality of School government was similarly far from simply negative; its rigidity had done much to suggest to a wider world that this was a mature and scholarly institution. But the rule of distinguished older men in suits certainly intimidated younger, untenured staff and was especially daunting for the small but growing number of women.

Philips should certainly be remembered as SOAS's greatest Director, even if his final years were ones in which the heavy demands of his Vice-Chancellorship of the University of London and his increasing profile in national public life meant that he could devote less time to the direction of SOAS. Some of his most significant achievements had been the product of his own capacious imagination and sheer hard work. Others had been the logical outcome of the massive expansion of higher education in the United Kingdom and the growing realization of the intellectual and practical significance of African and Asian studies. Enhanced official and public attention to Africa and Asia, the result of the attenuated end of colonial empires and the horror of the war in South East Asia, had powerfully validated the School's core concerns; and this in turn had probably guaranteed its long-term survival, a matter which the more pessimistic had episodically doubted before then.

That expansion had meant a growth in the numbers of academic staff. A flood of mostly younger teachers joined the School in the late 1960s and early 1970s. Most of the new appointees were products of the new national interest in African and Asian studies in western universities and, as such, few of them shared the backgrounds of their seniors, many of whom had arrived at their academic specialism after diplomatic, military or intelligence service before and during the Second World War. Whatever the proximate causes of these great changes, Philips was to be institutionally and personally remembered as a distinguished and humane modernizer, an expander and a developer. And while much of this had been achieved against considerable odds, his period in office was one of satisfying growth and one in which the School became better and better known in the outside world and increasingly capable of recruiting, retaining and producing first-class scholars. Philips was going to be an extremely tough act to follow.

The Cowan years

That task fell to another member of Philips's own department, the historian of modern South East Asia, Professor C. D. (Jeremy) Cowan. Beyond his success as a scholar, Cowan had already shown his considerable administrative flair as a constructive and emollient Dean of Students during the stormy era of the late 1960s in which some of the SOAS student body – and some of their teachers – had played a prominent role in the internationally widespread student unrest which was to greatly upset the usually calm Philips and many of the older members of the Senior Common Room. Cowan's inheritance was an undoubtedly lively and ambitious institution. While that might have been enviable, it also fell to him to begin to create a viable system of governance which could manage some of the results of a decade's uninhibited growth. SOAS had grown and its scholarly concerns had expanded well beyond the older focus of its functional and Orientalist beginnings. That this expansion changed the nature, and not just the size, of the institution was scarcely mirrored in its structure and especially its structures of governance.

At the heart of Cowan's dilemma lay a series of unresolved problems which stemmed from the fact that the School was still organized, formally and informally, as though it had remained a small, largely graduate and highly specialist institution in which everyone knew everyone else. Although there had been a decade's emphasis upon building up the 'modern' side of the School's work, SOAS was still politically dominated by its most senior figures most of whom had understandably been drawn from the 'classical' tradition. The 'classical' departments enjoyed, entirely justifiably, fine international reputations and for purely historical reasons boasted the majority of the professoriate. But it became increasingly clear that they had far fewer students than the brasher, *parvenu* social science departments; and this imbalance mattered more and more as it became increasingly clear that much of the School's funding hung on its capacity to increase the size of the student body. While logic suggested that the institution's political structure should evolve and thus match its significant thematic and even demographic change, its culture remained an occasionally charming and sometimes an authoritarian (even intimidating) mixture of high table, officers' mess and gentleman's club. Dominant figures were, as dominant figures will always be, slow to surrender privilege. Widening the membership of Academic Board, limiting the years for which any Head of Department might so serve and the opening-up of the processes which determined how new posts could be created – and how old posts could remain unfilled – were perceived as radical changes and Cowan was forced to struggle with older, senior and often internationally renowned colleagues who were, in turn, not slow to accuse him of being the philistine enemy of scholarly rectitude. At the same time he was also faced by an impatient cohort of younger, more recently appointed scholars, who were eager to expand their newly established fields by, for example, increasing staff numbers and library spending.

Although the competition for scarce resources and for the political authority to resist – or to carry-out – change is entirely healthy in any institution, SOAS's history of centralized authority meant that Cowan was inevitably seen, often unfairly, as hostile by the School's many interest groups. Perhaps there can be no better indication than this of his having carried out his role in a fair and principled fashion. But it was also unfair in that Cowan had considerably developed a tendency which had begun in the last years of Philips's tenure; Philips had come to share some of his burden with a small number of senior colleagues and this devolution became more formally established under Cowan. A sequence of academics – Stuart Simmonds, Charles Bawden and Adrian Mayer – was to support the Director as his deputy, the Pro-Director, in the years to come. And although their titles were to mutate with the same giddying frequency as those of British Departments of State, several senior scholars were to serve as Deans or Senior Tutors in the coming years (see Appendices). It was the beginning of something closer to Cabinet government at SOAS, an important shift away from the concentration of power which had characterized much of the period dominated by Philips and Bracken.

Cowan's period as Director witnessed the slow but challenging retreat of the central authority of the University of London and the taking over of the responsibility for much academic governance by the University's constituent schools and colleges. While the University's larger colleges and schools could relish their new–found autonomy and direct access to the national University Funding Council, the smallness of SOAS and the limited size and experience of its academic administration meant that its capacities were frequently stretched by this change. Now most undergraduate degrees were to be regulated and managed by schools and colleges rather than the University's committees and civil officers. As a consequence, a great many more functions fell upon the shoulders of the School's teachers and administrators. Issues like the determination of entry qualifications, course regulations, quality control and degree examinations had now to be managed by the School itself. Informality was increasingly a thing of the past and more and more staff time had to be devoted to work on a burgeoning number of committees. Individual teacher's filing cabinets were henceforward to be stuffed with vast amounts of paper as agendas, working papers and minutes piled up.

The slow retreat of the University of London was, however, to prove a relatively minor problem. Jeremy Cowan's programme of modernization was made even more urgent by the sudden deterioration of university funding in the United Kingdom. It became uncomfortably, even dramatically, obvious that the School's income and its special factor funding could not support the entirety of its teaching staff and its extensive programmes. With SOAS's long, proud tradition of attracting distinguished overseas students, the Government's decision to charge such students what it, arbitrarily, now determined was the 'economic fee', whilst continuing to subsidise those defined as 'home students', immediately harmed the School's recruitment especially at postgraduate level, and this obviously had a serious impact on fee income. A unique and growing institution with ambitious plans was at increasing risk of financial disaster.

There was almost certainly no way of surviving this crisis without surgery and it was Cowan's sad task to have to direct that surgery whilst doing his best to manage the resulting pain. In this Cowan was not alone as he was supported by a sequence of strong Pro-Directors. But the retirement of John Bracken in 1980, who had served as School Secretary for thirteen years, and then the sudden, unexpected death in office of his successor, Colin Moore in 1983, exposed the School's civil service at a critical time. The appointment of the widely liked and much respected Director of the School's External Services department, E. (Ted) O'Connor to the Secretaryship was to prove to be an outstanding success as O'Connor was able to maintain the affection and confidence of his colleagues for the following four years, a profoundly depressing time when people feared not only for their jobs but also for the futures of their fields.

It was, however, widely recognized that reform and regulation were essential, even if there was no agreement about the exact form of such changes. With the support of Academic Board and then Governing Body, in 1982 the Director set up a Working Party on Longer-term Development under the chairmanship of Malcolm Yapp, the Dean of Studies and an historian of the Near and Middle East. Although its remit was couched in suitably optimistic terms, it was clear that this Working Party would not only nominate areas in which growth should be encouraged (and hence funded), but would also determine which fields would necessarily stagnate or even die. Few had any illusions that this also meant early retirement for some teachers and the possibility of worse for others. Professional and personal fears meant that the long labours of the Working Party would be felt to be a divisive process and, however necessary it might have been, it was one which was doomed to make everybody unhappy.

This was the first time that the scholarly community at SOAS was confronted with the apparently uncaring and thoughtless implications of the market place. It was especially painful as the School's traditionally unworldly academic culture had habitually, if naively, regarded itself as above such crudities. It was a process which hardened, even coarsened, the institution and gave personal and departmental rivalries a harsher edge. Those who were to benefit from the exercise felt that they should have been more extensively favoured; those who were to lose out in the process of review deeply resented an implicitly judgmental process. This could be and was seen, however unfairly, as sometimes being arbitrary and as cravenly regarding scholarly significance as secondary to a field's capacity to attract large numbers of students. Involving as it did assumptions about an uncertain future, the Report of the Working Party was inevitably an uneven, imperfect plan. But the findings of the Yapp Report, as it became known, were to be used as a managerial template for many years to come. Posts in fields singled out as of significance or with potential would continue to be filled; those in fields regarded as more marginal or fading were not. In general, the number of teachers in the language and culture departments was to shrink dramatically in the coming years whilst those teaching on the School's 'modern' side were to grow; the Departments of Law, of Economics and Political Studies noticeably expanded.

It was Jeremy Cowan's – and Malcolm Yapp's – tragedy to be forever associated in the Senior Common Room's collective memory with the gratuitous instigation of savage 'cuts'. Like much folk memory, it is larded through with myth and cruel unfairness. Firstly, there is no doubt whatever that SOAS was living beyond its means and that one of the weaknesses of the previous two decades of growth had been a failure to think through how increasing expansion would have to be funded. For example, while the expansion of the School's teaching competence was undeniably exciting, its recurrent and increasing drain on the Library budget risked damaging the maintenance and growth of the core research collections for which the School enjoyed a deserved international reputation. And, secondly, it was frequently forgotten that Jeremy Cowan was only one of an extensive cohort of British vice-chancellors and principals who were also forced to initiate frequently painful programmes of retrenchment, which included early retirements, the freezing of posts and even the closure of departments, many of which were far more brutal than that endured by SOAS. The School's Director was no exception to the general rule that managing such processes invites a degree of profoundly felt, if often unreasonable, unpopularity. Throughout this exercise Cowan acted entirely democratically and always with the consent of the bodies working under the School's constitution, but it was still the worst of times.

Although the crisis was fundamentally about finance, Cowan had also recognized that there was a worrying lack of fit between the School of the 1980s and an administrative and political structure which in some respects went back fifty years. At the heart of that structure were the academic departments, the number of which had increased steadily since the 1960s; and these seemed likely to go on growing, a profound irony given that the financial crisis had actually reduced the numbers of the teaching staff. Appointment or election to the School's key committees recognized not only the importance of representation but also, implicitly, the equality of departments. Irrespective of the number of their students and teachers, departments were technically politically equal. Their relative autonomy ensured that they all had to have departmental heads, admissions tutors, departmental tutors, examination officers, as well as offices, secretaries and other discrete facilities; it was often forgotten that all these functions and spaces had to be paid for. The School supported not only a growing number of academic departments but also Area Studies Centres of which all teachers in the School were members. Centres, like departments, also demanded discrete office space and secretarial support as well as Chairs and MA programme convenors. The costs of all of this were considerable and were likely to continue mounting as there was constant demand for the increase in the number of departments and centres. Despite fears, the Yapp Report had not gone so far as to initiate the closure of any department or centre but had, rather, legitimated the designation of some fields, which had previously been contained within old-established departments, as potential departments in their own right. The School was simply too small to absorb what looked like an endless process of binary fission whose logical end was that every member of the School might be a formal and hence paid office-holder at either School, department or centre level. The inherent problems were laid before another Working Party on the Academic Organization of the School which was chaired by a distinguished historian and prominent member of the Governing Body, Professor D. A. Low, then Master of Clare Hall, Cambridge.

Quite what happened to the resulting Low Report is not entirely clear as it was mysteriously kicked into the long grass. It was a modest, reforming document which did little more than seek ways by which to rationalize the School's ramshackle political structure, a structure which had emerged rather than being rationally planned. Its conclusions were resisted by many of the teaching staff and, by failing to pursue it with anything like energy, by the School's management. The former were now almost certainly more inclined to defend narrow personal interests rather than conceiving of a wider institutional interest possibly because of the still raw scars left by the Yapp exercise: for them the Low enquiry was a reforming process too far. The latter seemed too exhausted by the struggles of recent years to engage in the further battles which would have been necessary to carry through a further tranche of reforms. The ultimate shelving of the Low Report's recommendations was a tragedy and delayed much-needed structural reform in the School by nearly twenty years.

The McWilliam period

From now onward the permanent concern of the School's management and especially its Governing Body and its Finance and General Purposes Committee was with finance, and part of the problem lay in the direct and indirect costs of an inappropriate structure. This almost certainly informed the Governing Body's decision to appoint Michael McWilliam to succeed Jeremy Cowan after thirteen years in what had become an increasingly hot seat. McWilliam was to be the first Director drawn from beyond the narrow confines of the university world. Although better known for his distinguished career in banking, McWilliam had begun his career as an applied economist and had more recently devoted a great deal of energy to maintaining the Royal African Society as, amongst other things, a bridge between academic study and commerce. There was a widespread awareness in the School that it had shown that it found it hard to manage itself. There was, accordingly, an expectation that a professional and, by repute, inspirational manager who had run a huge enterprise such as the Standard Chartered Bank might bring new ideas and new methods to re-shaping the School in preparation for the uncertainties of the next millennium.

There is no doubt that the advent of Michael McWilliam altered the managerial culture of the School for ever. At a personal level, his ebullient and unpretentious style – from now onwards first names were frequently to replace titles in exchanges in committee, for example – was very different from the somewhat austere and occasionally severe style of both Cyril Philips and Jeremy Cowan. As an outsider, McWilliam was clearly fascinated by the strange ways of those he had been appointed to direct. Like a good ethnographer, he noted the strengths as well as the weaknesses of the cultures and personalities of those he had come to work with while being amused or enraged by their eccentricities. As an outsider, he was able to recognize that the School was a potentially outstanding institution, not least because it was palpably distinctive and distinguished; its somewhat battered staff had lost sight of that in recent years. This was not simply a matter of low individual self-esteem. Partly because of the turbulence of recent years, the School's corporate self-presentation had been modest and defensive to the point of being almost absurdly self-effacing. So keen had the School been to demonstrate that it was every bit as respectable as any other British university that it had played down, even concealed, its particularities, many of which were, in fact, its strengths and which contributed towards its intriguing uniqueness. It was an institution which had grown up as a very small and rather odd member of the University of London and it had become unnecessarily deferential towards larger and, SOAS members seemed to feel, better-known, more famous colleges like the London School of Economics or University College.

Michael McWilliam was successful in raising the external profile of the School during his Directorship. With considerable imagination he – and his successor – used vacancies on the Governing Body to bring in new Governors who, unlike their predecessors, were not necessarily distinguished scholars but were, rather, significant figures from non-governmental organizations, from publishing, banking or international commerce. The involved concern of many of these new Governors helped in the task of proclaiming the relevance of SOAS and its work to a wider world. And the company of such interesting and important people helped McWilliam and his successor Sir Tim Lankester to inject some much needed and well-deserved doses of self-regard into their unnecessarily modest colleagues. The decade of the 1990s was certainly that during which members of the School could at last assume that people outside the limited world of the university would habitually recognize the initials SOAS, or even the word 'Soas', without having to spell out the institution's name in its tongue-twisting entirety.

Like all paranoid families, university communities tend to be suspicious of change and there was widespread suspicion that an outsider like McWilliam could have no understanding of what was variously understood to be the 'mission' of the School. That nervousness was to a very large extent lessened by the towering, even looming, presence of Professor John Wansbrough who had been Pro-Director since 1985. A very distinguished and internationally celebrated scholar, and coming as he did from one of the departments of language and culture on the 'classical' side of the School, Wansbrough was in a great many ways an ideal collaborator and foil for McWilliam. It was to prove a very strong combination but ended suddenly and somewhat mysteriously with Wansbrough's early resignation in 1992. This was a blow but McWilliam had built on precedent in making even more formal the notion of a management team. For four years he was assisted by not only a Pro-Director but also by three Deans, Tony Allan, John Peel and Richard Rathbone. Together with the Librarian, the Registrar, the Finance Officer and two senior but non-office-holding members of Academic Board, these were to constitute his Management Committee.

From different perspectives McWilliam and Wansbrough felt that further reform was essential if the School were to prosper. McWilliam set about modernizing the administrative structure of the School which was manifestly incapable of managing an institution which taught thousands of students, employed hundreds of people and spent millions of pounds of taxpayers' money every year. In this respect above all, the School looked absurdly amateurish in comparison with the private sector he had just relinquished. The School had, for example, not responded especially wisely to the coming of the new age of electronic information and many of its systems were relatively primitive. School statistics were frequently unreliable, often uninformative and inevitably late, and this made forward planning extremely difficult. Management requests for basic information took ages to complete. And there was a widely shared view that the School was unusually adept at the unending re-invention of the wheel. The long-overdue overhaul of much of this aspect of the School's governance, an absolute necessity in a new age which demanded transparency and accountability, was vital to survival. Radical changes of the sort that McWilliam and his Management Committee envisaged were, however, continually frustrated by two besetting problems which continue to haunt the School.

Firstly the academic members of the School were stridently resistant to the spending of any more of the School's limited finances on administration rather than upon things more obviously associated with research or teaching. Perversely perhaps, academics everywhere complain about the increasing administrative burdens they are forced to bear but resist the costs associated with the lifting of those burdens. Those costs are partly financial; but they also involve the partial loss of control over a variety of decisions which academics regard as part of their strongly defended notion of academic freedom. Secondly, national employment legislation and the nature of most employment contracts meant that reform depended upon persuading administrative post-holders to perform in different ways. In some cases this proved difficult. So far as administrators were concerned the School had to compete in a job market increasingly dominated by a high paying, booming City. It was hard to recruit and even harder to retain first-rate administrative staff.

The academic modernizing agenda largely overseen by John Wansbrough concerned the School's scholarly output. With no sense of pleasure, he and the School's managers recognized that the times were changing and that universities would soon be challenged by the creation of an extensive system of national review and audit. The School's teaching capacity would now be examined by intrusive panels of inspectors set up by a government agency. Success in such peer-reviews would hang in part upon good record-keeping as well as pedagogic dynamism in the classroom. That meant that the sometimes charming but obviously anachronistic habits of what had once been a face-to-face society, but was now a fast-growing teaching institution, simply would no longer meet the bill. Mutual trust, reliance upon inspiration and the back of the envelope were things of the past. Wansbrough and a succession of undergraduate and postgraduate Deans forced through a series of reforms which certainly increased the burden of bureaucracy upon teachers and magnified the sheer volume of paper, but they did so out of necessity.

The School's research was also now to be peer reviewed by Research Assessment Exercises. Universities had been funded for research and now government declared that it wished to examine the quantity and quality of that research. Although the School had a distinguished record of research publication by outstanding scholars, Wansbrough detected in some of his colleagues a lack of urgency. The new urgency was occasioned by the fact that research quality and quantity was soon to be scored and that only high scores would confer the mantle of excellence as well as bringing in much-needed research revenue from the State. Wansbrough's monitoring of the School's research effort and the resulting arm-twisting felt intrusive to many of the academic staff who felt mistrusted. It was, however, merely the local manifestation of the beginnings of a far more widespread nosy and *dirigiste* culture in British universities.

The achievements of McWilliam and his Pro-Directors Wansbrough and R. H. (Bob) Taylor, who took over from Wansbrough in 1992, were considerable. Modernization was apparent in the generation of serious things like Strategic Plans and Mission Statements and in the slightly lighter form of the design of a School logo. In general terms, McWilliam and Wansbrough presided over an institution whose members exuded increasing confidence and self-regard. While such emotions are invisible, those sentiments were to be echoed in the more tangible form of the Brunei building. An exceptionally generous grant from the Sultan of Brunei allowed the School to colonize the wasteland to the south of the main building which still boasted the asbestos-lined huts used by the builders who had put up Senate House just before the outbreak of the Second World War. The handsome new building was to answer some, but far from all, of the School's pressing needs for accommodation. The hunt for teaching and office space in the centre of one of the most expensive cities on the planet has probably been the most significant continual theme in the history of the School. But it created a fine new lecture theatre, some well-equipped teaching rooms, a roof garden with what developers call 'potential', as well as, in its two floors of galleries, some of the best new dedicated exhibition space in central London. It did all of this in a beautiful brick building whose detail and proportion complement not only the under-rated elegance of both Birkbeck and SOAS's 1930s listed buildings but also the Georgian buildings to its south and the terra-cotta clad buildings to its north in Russell Square. Having lost the old hutments and the car-park, SOAS now straddled a precinct whose good looks have been enhanced as the small, recently planted avenue of trees has become mature.

If the School was cheered by its increasingly pleasant location and the great generosity which lay behind this enhancement, its besetting problems persisted and some new ones intruded. The emergence of intolerant religious fundamentalism on the campus led to a disgraceful and frightening occupation of the offices of the Director and Secretary whilst they were physically there. But this unpleasantness drew the School

SOAS from Senate House

Sir Cyril Philips examining plans for the new building

Students relaxing outside the College Building

Members of the Governing Body, June 2002

(Front row, left to right): Sir Joseph Hotung, Dr Bengisu Rona, Mr Jonathan Taylor, Professor Colin Bundy, The Lord Bagri, Dr David Khalili, Professor Elisabeth Croll

(Back row, left to right): Sir David John, Professor Christopher Shackle, Dr William Radice, Dr Cathy Jenkins, Mr Peter Collecott, Mr Samuel Jonah, Mr Liam Frost, Professor Ruth Finnegan, Professor Ian Brown, Ms Jo Halliday (Secretary), Mr Frank Dabell (Clerk), The Hon Barbara Thomas

The Dalai Lama at SOAS with Sir Michael McWilliam

The President of the Republic of Korea, Mr. Kim Dae-jung,
and his wife, with Professor Martina Deuchler, at SOAS in 1998

The opening of the Vernon Square campus in October 2001:
the Director and Principal, Professor Colin Bundy,
with HRH Princess Anne, the Princess Royal, Chancellor of the University of London,
Councillor Joe Trotter, Mayor of Islington, and the Visitor, Lord Howe of Aberavon

HRH the Emir of Katsina in the Library in 1996

Outside the College Building

together and led to the drafting of an admirable statement about academic freedom to which all members of the School are now required to subscribe. The more abiding problems were financial and structural. While a great deal of progress was registered in terms of increased numbers and levels of research grants, rising numbers of students and earnings from various forms of consultancy, the fee per student paid by the Higher Education Funding Council for England (HEFCE) declined in real as well as in money terms. Maintaining the Library while book and cataloguing costs rocketed forced unwelcome choices upon staff. Now they were frequently asked to nominate the periodical or journal they would be prepared to sacrifice if the new journal they proposed was to be purchased. And the increasing use of the new technology in research and learning imposed new financial burdens in terms of hardware, software and the expertise needed to maintain it. As ever the School was asked to either increase its income or make economies. The former tactic proved elusive not least because successful academic entrepreneurship requires teachers to set aside time for planning, to use seed money and to use support staff. By the 1990s SOAS could afford none of these luxuries.

Economizing proved to be a no less elusive goal. Quite what could be and should be cut was endlessly debated but predictably, of course, there were no volunteers. Attempts to rationalize the administration of the Masters degree programmes in the operation of a Graduate School were only partly successful and suggestions of departmental mergers were hotly resisted. When McWilliam and his Management Committee agreed to attempt to wind up the School's Linguistics Department, this proposal was successfully defeated in an extended meeting of the Academic Board. The need for change was widely understood but there was no agreement about the nature of that change. Towards the end of the McWilliam era, Academic Board once again initiated a working party to discuss structural change.

The major achievement of all the post-war Directors was, however, to lead the School into a position where it was regarded by the outside world as indispensable and thus worthy of support. Under Jeremy Cowan the School had sufficiently impressed Sir Peter Parker to make the report he had been asked to make by government on the significance of Asian and African languages for the commercial and diplomatic future of the country one which strongly supported the School's mission. In 1993, during McWilliam's stewardship, the School was even more directly observed and the resulting Raisman Report was no less supportive of much of what the School sought to achieve. It is almost certain that without such persuasive public plaudits, the readiness of HEFCE to recognize the need for Special Factor Funding for the unique but important concerns of the School might have been less apparent.

Recent years

Financially, the School's survival has rested in no small measure upon the masterly running of what is somewhat portentously referred to as the School's Estate. This owed a great deal to the sheer originality of Frank Dabell, the School's Secretary from 1993 to 2002. Dabell's understanding of the property market and the law has allowed the School to profit in the form of two much-needed student halls of residence and a new campus near both of these halls on the borders of Islington. The purchase and then sale of the halls whilst retaining them as student residences successfully financed what would otherwise have been a very damaging deficit. The School's debt to Frank Dabell, a man whose post inevitably attracts more brick-bats than applause, is as great if not greater than it is to its recent Directors.

Each of the three Directors so far considered enjoyed early success, then struggled to maintain momentum for change in their 'middle periods' and finally endured an endgame when a degree of political weakness was underlined by the fact that it was clear that they were on the brink of retirement. Following a false start, the Governing Body's Search Committee recommended the appointment of another non-academic Director to succeed McWilliam in 1996. Sir Tim Lankester had enjoyed a successful career in the civil service which, usefully from the SOAS point of view, had included periods in both the Department of Education and that of Overseas Development. Aware of the absolute need for continuity, the Pro-Director, Professor Bob Taylor, generously stayed in post for a term before taking up the Vice-Chancellorship of the University of Buckingham as Sir Tim acquainted himself with the ways of the School. Sir Tim was also supported by the continuing service of Frank Dabell and eventually by Professor Christopher Shackle, the Pro-Director for Academic Affairs from 1997 to 2003. A formidable scholar and Fellow of the British Academy, Shackle's contribution to the School recalls that of John Wansbrough. His management of the academic life of the School was, however, to be far more universally admired because of its palpable fairness and imagination. This had a great deal to do with Shackle's humour and human decency as well as his great intelligence.

Lankester and his closest advisors adjusted the portfolios of those who had formally been called Deans but were now renamed Pro-Directors. There was a clearer identification with development in the appointment of the economist Laurence Harris as the Pro-Director for Research amongst whose tasks were to be the facilitation of the research of staff and students and the management of the School's submission to the second Research Assessment Exercise (RAE). Although the management of teaching was briefly shared between two Pro-Directors, these two posts were fused in the exceptionally onerous task of the Pro-Directorship for Taught Courses. This extensive role was taken on and in many respects was created *de novo* by David Taylor between 1999 and 2002. With great political skill, Taylor persuaded a reluctant School that order was preferable to chaos, even if that threatened some of the strange Spanish customs which departments had defended *à l'outrance*. Much of this work was decidedly unglamorous but was an essential preparation for the era of mass teaching into which the School was now entering. David Arnold took over the Pro-Directorship for Research in 1999. A highly productive historian with an enviable international reputation, he demonstrated a very constructive approach to the facilitation of research and an entirely justified intolerance of those who promised much but failed to deliver. Unsurprisingly, the RAE for which he prepared the School in 2001 yielded the highest research ratings thus far. With Christopher Shackle this was to prove to be a formidable team.

Tim Lankester used his relatively short period in office in a serious attempt to further underline the immediate relevance and importance of the School's studies. Using his excellent contacts in the worlds of politics and international affairs, Lankester was keen to have the School's activities closely engaged with and observed by 'opinion makers' whilst ensuring that SOAS had an increasingly realistic sense of how important it was for its survival to enjoy a reputation as a modern-minded, relevant institution. But Sir Tim was faced, as had been his predecessors, with a host of mainly financial problems. He put a good deal of effort into attempts to improve the School's surprisingly poor record of fundraising. Despite strenuous efforts, including the brief employment of public relations and fundraising expertise, the returns were disappointing. The problem was, once again, the scale of the School. It was, and is, too small to afford the dedicated fundraising departments which many larger institutions use to badger both their alumni and those potentially generous people who wish to be associated with great institutions. For this reason perhaps Lankester's attempt to create just such an office in the School disappointingly failed to pay its way; some critics argued that it was always too small a venture whilst others argued that such enterprises take years to show results. But even while this initiative was being withdrawn, the Director and others continued to work hard on the generation of external funding and donations and not without some success.

IT WAS TIMES LIKE THESE WHEN SIR TIM FAIRLY RELISHED HIS REPUTATION AS AN OLD CHARMER

Sir Tim Lankester

During Sir Tim Lankester's Directorship, which ended with the millennium when he took up office as President of Corpus Christi College, Oxford, in 2001, the School was once again to be preoccupied with the consideration of a new structural model devised by a working party established by the Academic Board which promised to reduce the expense of administration by streamlining it. This laid out a sensible reforming strategy that respected the sensitivities of the teaching staff and proposed nothing which seriously compromised intellectual or personal integrity. Having, it seems, learnt nothing from its last flirtation with this crucial issue, Academic Board again dodged the issue. Clearly the plan included necessary proposals for internal merger and synergy but these were widely read as unacceptable threats to departmental or even personal autonomy; and to convince people otherwise would have required a good deal of effort in the form of political preparation, effort which was quite simply missing. Ultimately the effect was merely to postpone structural change.

Under Tim Lankester the School had developed a new style of government whereby formally at least the academic life of the School was run by a senior academic whilst the numerous other concerns were managed by the Director. Rational as this was, the continued existence of the School as, in effect, a huge federation, or rather a federation of a large number of uneven units, clearly had no future. Far too much academic staff time was taken up in repetitive, wasteful work which reduced the hours available for research or teaching. Insisting that a more cost-effective structure must be adopted was a task that was to fall to Lankester's successor, the internationally respected historian of southern Africa, Professor Colin Bundy. He has already ushered in what is certainly the most dramatic change in the School's government in its long history. The cornerstones of identity and political power for so many decades in the history of the School, the departments, have been abandoned in favour of three faculties each of which is presided over by a Dean and a Faculty Board. At the time of writing it is too early to assess the success of this dramatic and brave reform. But as the School is once again faced with one of its periodic financial crises, the new faculty structure may provide the Director and his Deans with a more rational system with which to navigate these new rapids.

4

Language studies: A play in three acts

Christopher Shackle

Prologue

The unique character of SOAS has always been closely linked to the peculiarly prominent place within the School of language studies. It is true that these studies have long since ceased to have the quite overwhelming institutional dominance which they formerly enjoyed, both for better and for worse, over the narrower academic profile of the School's earlier decades. But the study of language and of languages continues to be the core defining function of six of the historic departments of SOAS: besides the Department of Phonetics and Linguistics, recently re-named the Department of Linguistics, these are the five regionally arranged Departments of Languages and Cultures, respectively of East Asia, of South East Asia and Islands, of South Asia, of the Near and Middle East, and of Africa. Accounting for a majority of the School's staff at the beginning of the period covered by this chapter, these departments still contain a third of the academic faculty.

Few if any other university institutions in any country contain this exceptionally high proportion of language specialists, still less so many specialists in Asian and African languages. Although its overall institutional share of the British higher education sector is reckoned at 0.1 per cent, SOAS has the equivalent of more than 60 full time research active academic staff in these languages, which is over a quarter of the national total. This massive specialist tilt has had a number of important implications for the School's definition and development.

Internally, the historic profile of the five regional departments has influenced not only the set-up of the School's Library with its regionally administered collections, but also the typical internal organization of most other academic departments. These have primarily defined by discipline but have generally sought to replicate within themselves the same five-fold regional coverage, typically on what might be called the Noah's Ark principle of at least two disciplinary specialists per region. Perceived tensions between disciplinary and regional coverage have thus in different ways characterized all the disciplinary departments. In the case of language-based studies, similar tensions have typically been played out, at SOAS as elsewhere, in the polarities between those who for the purposes of this chapter are labelled 'linguisticians' primarily interested in language and 'linguists' primarily interested in one or more languages and the distinctive literatures and cultures associated with them. No more absolute here than anywhere else, these polarities have tended to define the relationship between the Department of Phonetics and Linguistics on the one hand and the five Departments of Languages and Cultures on the other. The sometimes awkward working out of this relationship thus forms a significant sub-plot in the narrative of this chapter, which is itself made intrinsically complex enough by the academic particularism which is a natural characteristic of language and culture specialists everywhere, including the SOAS linguists who have always heavily outnumbered the linguisticians.

Blessed by a long tradition of institutional rhetoric which happily emphasizes the harmony of its complementary parts, SOAS has nevertheless experienced for just as long an inherent tension between the five regional Departments of Languages and Cultures and all the other disciplinary departments. Due in part to the different bases of their definition, this has been played out against a cyclical struggle with external pressures, particularly those stemming from the sheer cost of maintaining the integrity of a uniquely precious collective resource of language-based expertise on Asia and Africa which is hardly paralleled anywhere else in the world. Over the last thirty years, this has been a recurrent issue for all Directors, none of whom has been either a linguist or a linguistician, and for whom the SOAS language portfolio has as often as not constituted a recurrent financial problem quite as much as a distinctive academic glory. It has, as from the School's earliest days, regularly involved SOAS looking to central funding agencies for special support in the national interest. All this has had its own impact on the development of regional departments, whose members have at the same time been experiencing the effects of the wider shift in attitudes towards the study of languages amongst British university students over the last generation, even if they have not always been conscious of the close parallels with the experience of their Europeanist colleagues.

The story of language studies at SOAS is both too complex and too bitty to be told fully or easily, and is here deliberately simplified by treating the five regional departments as a composite whole. Other omissions of detail have been necessitated by the frequent uncertainty of the record and by the need for great compression. The chapter is given narrative shape as a drama with a deliberately limited cast of named players. It comprises three acts, opening with artificial sunlight streaming through the french windows on to one of those well-appointed interiors of yesteryear, followed by the gloomy setting of a grimly realist second act, and rounded off by finale which with the help of some theatrical magic succeeds in ending on a genuinely upbeat note.

Act I: Coverage and contentment

Dhanyānāṃ girikandare nivasatāṃ
jyotiḥ paraṃ dhyāyatām

How favoured you are to sit in mountain caves
to meditate upon an inner light
Bhartrihari

The 1960s are now rightly celebrated as the heyday of Philips's period as Director, during which he used the new resources made available by the Hayter Report of 1961 for the development of the social sciences and the founding of the regional Centres. But in that decade and through to the 1970s, the language-based Departments of the School still reflected in their strengths and weaknesses the legacy of the immediate post-war period during which Turner, himself Professor of Sanskrit and the last of the School's Directors to come from the language side, had used the generous funding provided after the Scarbrough Report of 1946 to build up impressive numbers of language specialists. This is a period of golden reminiscence for most of those who experienced the exceptionally privileged conditions which were then made possible by extraordinarily generous funding. There was freedom from external accountability and, given the very low student numbers, freedom from substantial teaching commitments, permitting a largely untrammelled cultivation of the academic life which could lead equally to the extremes of formidable scholarship and to the limits of professorial eccentricity. In some cases these were combined in a single individual, most famously perhaps in C. E. Bazell, the archetypally absent-minded Professor of Linguistics of whom Ruth Kempson's obituary recalls: 'he was probably the most brilliant mind London linguistics has known, but his total quite undeliberate eccentricity prevented all but the few who had the privilege of working under him from recognizing his worth.'

The Department of Phonetics and Linguistics, with 13 members of staff in 1966, had established a major external presence for SOAS under the earlier leadership of J. R. Firth in the then quite new discipline of linguistics. Within the School, too, Firth's exceptional position had ensured a high profile for the department vis-à-vis the five departments of languages and cultures, which then embraced over two-thirds of the academic faculty. In the order in which they were then listed in the School Calendar, pride of imperial place was given to the India Department (with 21 members of staff), followed by the Departments of South East Asia (13), of the Far East (23), of the Near and Middle East (30), and of Africa (25).

The academic culture of these departments was still unambiguously dominated by the high Orientalist tradition, which was itself a nineteenth century extension of Western classical scholarship. Its leading practitioners combined great learning with grand schemes which were formidably conceived and executed. If one was looking for a single monument to the outstanding achievements which the SOAS regional departments were capable of at their best it would be hard to find a more apt illustration than Sir Ralph Turner's *A Comparative Dictionary of the Indo-Aryan Languages*. First published in 1966 and in print ever since, this massive volume of over 800 pages remains an indispensable guide to the etymologies and the historical linguistics of the Indo-Aryan language family, containing some 140,000 entries arranged under Sanskritic etyma. The size, the ambition, the scholarship are equally remarkable, as is the astonishing ability of Turner to keep going, first as Professor of Sanskrit, then through his long Directorship, to bring finally to the point of completion in his seventies the great work which he had first conceived some fifty years earlier while on military service in the First World War as a work of reference which would do for the Indo-Aryan languages derived from Sanskrit what W. Meyer-Lübke's classic *Romanisches Etymologisches Wörterbuch* (1911-19) had done for the Romance languages derived from Latin.

This great scholarly tradition continued to be practised at the highest level by the leading members of the serving staff of the regional departments, whose professoriate in 1966 included five of the School's seven Fellows of the British Academy. Two were shortly to leave, the Indologist John Brough for Cambridge and the Sinologist Denis Twitchett for the United States, while the other three were to continue distinguished careers at SOAS until their retirement in the 1970s. These were the Assyriologist Donald Wiseman, the Ethiopianist Edward Ullendorff, and the Persian scholar and historian of Iran Ann Lambton, whose special presence in the School is recalled in Hugh Baker's chapter.

Admittedly not all the faculty were up to this formidable standard. The penny-pinched regional departments of the pre-war period had been spectacularly expanded, as the financial resources which resulted from the implementation of the Scarbrough Committee's recommendations were used in Turner's period for a huge extension of language coverage, more or less irrespective of demand. Besides providing opportunities for conventionally trained younger scholars, this massive expansion of the departments over quite a short period had drawn in recruits to academic life from wartime service experience or the colonial education services, for many of whom the Scarbrough scheme of Treasury Studentships offered retraining. Firth had seen to it that all new recruits to the regional departments had a compulsory year or two of training in the Department of Phonetics and Linguistics, a practice which continued until the early 1960s and which continued to be resented by some of those who had experienced it until their retirements.

The level of training provided within the regional departments themselves to their junior faculty seems to have been a more erratic affair. From the rapid expansion of staff numbers there resulted the presence for a whole generation of a collection of personalities who might in charitable retrospect be termed interdisciplinarians *ante litteram*, or in a word charming scholars of the old school who used the ample leisure which the terms of their employment then afforded them to pursue a variety of interests more or less plausibly justified by their language specialisms. It must be said that the abundant resources of those years were not always put to the most productive scholarly use, and it is sad to reflect on all those unwritten grammars and dictionaries which might have been produced for the later benefit of more hard-pressed generations.

It should also be observed that as well as languages a broad range of cultural phenomena including, besides literature, also religion and philosophy, art and archaeology and music then formed a full part of the remit of the regional departments, and so the spread of individual academics' interests was ultimately beneficial to the expansion of the School's range of offerings. Some with particular interests in these fields played their part in the relevant University Boards of Studies. But little exposure to the outside academic world was required of most academics in the regional departments, since the London University Board of Studies in Oriental and African Languages and Literatures was itself effectively an extension of SOAS. So the regional departments were on the whole very agreeable rather than intellectually very exciting places to be.

The level of that agreeability did depend very much upon the personality of the Head of Department, at that period normally a Professor who might continue in that role for decades and who consequently had the real power to make or break careers. Very powerful figures in their own right, some of the Heads of Departments of Languages and Cultures were determined to maintain their historic primacy over the new disciplines being fostered in the 1960s. Philips's autobiography vividly records the bitter feelings evoked by the opposition to his changes mounted by the Heads of the India and Africa Departments: 'It was the two professorial prima donnas, John Brough and Malcolm Guthrie, the former opinionated in the overriding value of intellect, the latter a former missionary in West Africa convinced that God was always on his side, who posed a serious threat. They were determined to go on enlarging their already overgrown language departments, thus pre-empting all hope from school funds of diversifying our studies.' In fact, by 1966 Philips had won the battle, and the numbers of staff in regional departments were not to expand further, although they were quite large enough for most to be content to remain within their boundaries, and notably few were, for instance, to serve as Chairs of Regional Centres.

Students were certainly still rather few and far between. There were some overseas research students, especially from India and other Commonwealth countries, but the numbers of British undergraduates were very small. Registered for the old-fashioned single-subject degrees of the day, in which everything was decided by the final examination at the end of the course, with carefully prescribed papers involving a heavy emphasis on written translation and including plenty of set texts drawn from the literature of earlier periods, only 27 BA students graduated from the regional departments in 1966-67, with 6 each in Arabic and Chinese, 2 each in Hausa, Swahili, Japanese, Persian, Sanskrit and Turkish, and 1 each in Hebrew and Assyrian, Hindi, and Malay. As always, the demand was greatest for introductory courses, and much mechanical industry went into the production of internally circulated elementary language materials, often of pretty amateurish quality. These, it must be remembered, were the days of the manual typewriter and of reproduction by stencil. Even though departments possessed ingeniously customized keyboards with phonetic characters distributed here and there in the less-used corners of the qwertyuiop layout, this state of affairs caused great problems for those devising Asian and African language teaching materials.

Throughout the 1970s there was considerable staff stability within the language departments. This may be attributed to the expanded recruitment of the post-war period, and to the lack of alternative employment opportunities for most, other than the exceptionally talented who were recruited to the United States or sometimes to Oxbridge, not to speak of the excellent working conditions of the period which encouraged staying put. Nor did the relatively small number of new recruits offer a challenge to successfully established patterns. Scholarly tradition continued to be reflected in the pages of the School's *Bulletin*, whose Editorial Board was chaired for most of the decade by Edward Ullendorff, himself an outstanding representative of that tradition, which was also maintained in monograph form in the London Oriental Series and other specialist titles subsidized by the Publications Committee. Gratitude for this necessary financial support was seldom more gracefully acknowledged than by Harry Shorto, himself often referred to as a practitioner of the ultimate in exotic scholarly specialism, in the preface to his *Dictionary of the Mon Inscriptions from the Sixth to the Sixteenth Centuries* (1971): 'It is far from being the sum of my gratitude to an institution which has provided a matrix for the nurturing of such studies scarcely paralleled elsewhere.' A similarly protected specialist outlet for the work of many of SOAS's numerous Africanists was found within the orange covers of *African Language Studies*. It was a while before the challenge of Edward Said's *Orientalism* (1974) was to be seriously felt, and anyway that contentious book's chief SOAS target was the historian Bernard Lewis, himself due to leave for the United States in the same year.

In terms of administrative leadership, too, this was a period in which there was rather little change among the Heads of Departments, whose term of office was not yet fixed. In Philips's last period and much of Cowan's Directorship, the Headships of the regional departments were filled for many years at a stretch by Clifford Wright (Indology and South Asia 1969-83), Stuart Simmonds (South East Asia 1966-82), Charles Bawden (Far East 1970-84), Ann Lambton (Near and Middle East 1971-78), and Edward Ullendorff (Africa 1971-77). The longest period of all was served by R.H. 'Bobby' Robins (Phonetics and Linguistics 1969-85), whose combination of intellectual distinction with a notably affable personality did so much to ensure the standing of the department in the wider world of linguistics as well as internally harmonious relationships.

It was possible in those years for the pace of change to be kept quite slow, and for hierarchical structures to remain very much in place. Although there were certainly tensions between the regional departments originally funded by Scarbrough on the one hand and the disciplinary departments substantially expanded by Hayter on the other, there was sufficient resource in the system for the accommodation of the different cultures which these embodied. The importance within the School of the language departments was recognized by the appointment of Simmonds from 1973 to the Deanship, the second position in the School's hierarchy. In 1981 he was re-designated Pro-Director, a post which in the following year passed to Bawden until 1984.

There were some changes. Although undergraduate student numbers remained very low in the regional departments, there was a gradual shift towards making the School's languages available to greater numbers of students through the introduction of modular degrees examined by course units, and in Phonetics and Linguistics, close co-operation with University College allowed an active programme of Masters teaching and research supervision. The departmental structure remained very much in placed throughout, although the 1970s did see the first steps being taken towards the separate definition of several humanities subjects with the formation of Panels and Centres for Art and Archaeology and for Music, which drew almost entirely upon the members of the departments of languages and cultures, and for Religion and Philosophy, where they played a significant part alongside a leadership derived from the Department of History.

Act II: Crises and contractions

Pesa sasimbua roho yangu

Money is the root of all my problems
Swahili song

The Thatcher years were to be a time of traumatic change for many hitherto comfortably padded corners of British national life, and SOAS language studies were certainly no exception. Severe cuts to the comfortable pattern of support which the School had enjoyed as the result of generously top-sliced funding distributed through the University were suddenly threatened. One of the Thatcher Government's first measures was to raise the fees payable by overseas postgraduate students, a move with particularly serious consequences for SOAS with its historically high proportion of such students. This was shortly followed by general cuts in the funding of British universities. The impact of these measures fell most heavily upon the regional departments, since retrenchments would clearly have to fall upon the economically least viable parts of the School, which were concentrated in these departments with their still ample staffing and still small student numbers.

The vulnerability of SOAS to Thatcherite change thus had particularly important consequences for the regional departments, who experienced a disorienting period of shock involving a quite serious contraction in staff numbers. For those who remained there was a strong challenge to their sense of an historically justified central place within the School and much uncertainty about their future development. In comparison to the confidence which had characterized the preceding period, this was a time of uncertain and often inward looking defensiveness within the language departments, at worst of a paranoia helplessly directed against the School's management and the direction in which it was leading.

Since this was also the time when many of those recruited to the regional departments after the war were themselves approaching the later part of their careers, the challenges of adaptation to a changed climate proved less attractive to many than the quite generous provisions of a centrally funded early retirement scheme, and SOAS staff numbers were quite sharply reduced, especially in these departments. The record shows that the enduring folk memory of a sudden decimation is not entirely accurate, but the painful scale of contraction may be gauged by the comparison of departmental staff complements for the academic year 1976-77 with those for 1986-87, when the Department of South Asia had been reduced from 17 to 15.5, South East Asia from 16 to 8, the Far East from 24 to 19, the Near and Middle East from 27 to 19, Africa from 17 to 10 and Phonetics and Linguistics from 13 to 8.5. From a total of 114, itself virtually the same as the 112 detailed above for 1966-67, down to only 80, this represents an overall reduction by nearly a third over ten years.

In the handling of this massive internal contraction an important strategic role in considering its implications for the School's future development was played by the Working Party on Longer-term Development which was established in 1982. Chaired by Malcolm Yapp as Dean of Studies, the Working Party was made up of six middle-ranking members of academic staff, including three from the regional departments. For those of us involved, this was an extraordinary opportunity to gain a first hand impression of the work of the School at this crucial period of change. It was a major exercise, involving 29 often lengthy meetings throughout a warm summer term, and comprising a total of some 120 hours of which at least 90 hours were devoted to face-to-face meetings with all available members of the academic staff.

Many of these meetings were with members of the regional departments, for the Yapp Working Party recognized that these departments were collocations of subjects rather than coherent disciplinary units, as the Hayter Report had recognized but as had hardly been factored into the internal self-conception of the School, still less of its Heads of Departments Committee. For the first time an attempt was made to correlate the planning of staffing numbers with likely teaching needs, rather than with the loftier considerations of language coverage or of the abstract needs of pure scholarship which an earlier regime had allowed to be so freely advanced. So it was that a rough rule of thumb was evolved by the Working Party for distinguishing between major languages capable of providing a full undergraduate degree, those for which a half degree would be the optimum offering, and others from which only single units could be expected. In order to avoid Asian or African connotations, these three categories were arbitrarily given North American labels, and were respectively described as 'Sioux', 'Apache' and 'Cherokee' languages. Although the labels predictably met with their fair share of mockery at the time, the thinking behind the scheme has proved to be of continuing influence and utility in deciding the pattern of subsequent appointments.

The longer-term development envisaged by the Yapp Working Party was hardly very encouraging for the regional departments, since yet further reductions in their staffing were envisaged over time, with a total projected complement of only 57, plus 10 for Phonetics and Linguistics. As before, however, the same special character of SOAS's unique mission for Asian and African languages which had caused the crisis was also invoked to save it. In 1985 Sir Peter Parker, a business leader with a particular interest in Japan, was commissioned to undertake a one-man review of the requirements of diplomacy and commerce for Asian and African languages and area studies. Conceived in part as a sort of mini-update of the Hayter Report, though excluding from its remit that report's comprehensive attention to academic needs, the Parker Report when published in February 1986 made a robust case for additional resources to be given to language posts which would in part offset the deleterious consequences of the recent cuts at SOAS and elsewhere.

The School received the lion's share of the funding which flowed from the acceptance of the report, and this was particularly valuable for the future development of the School's language departments through enabling the establishment of Training Fellowships to bring in much needed new blood.

Along with these two very significant reports, a number of general trends may be observed to have characterized the period. It became the practice from the early 1980s no longer to appoint permanent Heads of Department as these positions fell vacant, but rather acting Heads who would expected to served for fixed terms of four years in a development which made for greater internal consultation than had hitherto always been the case. The internal character of the regional departments itself became less diverse during this period, and their staff numbers were progressively reduced as the subject centres successfully established for the various arts and humanities disciplines were converted into full departments of their own. As is described in the following chapter, this process began with the establishment of the Department of Art and Archaeology in 1990, followed by the Study of Religions in 1992. Although the Centre of Music Studies was the oldest of all, having been established in 1979, its movement to a Department was delayed by its small size until 1998. New ideas also began to emerge for other cross-regional groupings, for instance for the study of literature or film. These were much encouraged, if not to immediate fruition, by John Wansbrough, Head of the Department of the Near and Middle East since 1982 and the major voice of the regional departments in the School during his period as Pro-Director from 1985 to 1992.

Besides the pattern of retirements of older members of staff, the notably greater emphasis on modern studies which came during this period to be characteristic of the School, as of all other institutions sensitive to changing student expectations, led to a significant weakening of pre-modern studies across the board, with the notable exception of a distinguished team of specialists in Ancient Near Eastern languages. The overlapping gradual reorientation of the regional departments away from the narrower kinds of philological and linguistic concern which had long preoccupied many of their members may be symbolized by the closure of *African Language Studies* and its replacement by the departmental *Journal of African Languages and Cultures*, which recently was itself tellingly re-entitled as the *Journal of African Cultural Studies*.

Although less narrowly tied than in earlier years to the publication of SOAS staff research, the *Bulletin of SOAS* continued in its special relationship to the regional departments under Wansbrough's able chairmanship of the Editorial Board and with the much valued support over twenty years from 1979 of its Editorial Secretary Diana Matias, in succession to Doris Johnson's long tenure of this post. The School's Publications Committee, serviced with devoted skill for many years by Martin Daly, also continued to fulfil its useful role as 'publisher of last resort' in encouraging the publication of the more recondite items of staff research, particularly on the language side, for which the market would always be very small. The pattern of individuals' publications was much the same as it had long been, with a primary mix of teaching grammars, linguistic descriptions and literary studies, along with the particular focus on area studies characteristic of those academics within the language and culture departments who felt a natural affinity with the work of the Area Centres. With the notable exception of the Department of Phonetics and Linguistics, which had always been actively tied into an international disciplinary network, most of the School's language departments remained fairly inward-turned, though perhaps no more so than many foreign language departments in British universities during the period. Certainly, there was no very conspicuous embrace at that time of the new theoretical emphases which were coming to characterize literary and cultural studies in Europe and the English-speaking academic world. The first Research Assessment Exercise of 1989 hardly provides more than the bare data for judging the consequences of this conservatism, since members of the regional departments were submitted along the rest of the School's faculty for an embarrassingly disappointing rating of 3 under a general area studies rubric.

Many of the posts without significant teaching duties lapsed with the cuts of early 1980s. In the working life of most members of the regional departments, there was now a much greater emphasis upon the teaching of students – especially of undergraduates, given the difficulty of attracting serious numbers of qualified graduate students to more advanced programmes demanding a high level of competence in difficult languages. Collaboration with other departments was partially encouraged by the growth in two-subject degrees, which was of great significance for most languages whose staffing did not permit them to run viable degrees of their own.

Economies forced the need for a greater attention to more professional methods and delivery of language teaching. From the late 1980s there was an increasing diversion of some departmental resource from the appointment of research active academic staff into the appointment of teaching-only language lectors. Pioneered by the Japanese section, and soon followed by Chinese and Arabic, this development was to the great benefit of teaching programmes, especially in the major languages. New problems for handling different levels of prior linguistic competence as well as new opportunities were created by the recruitment of significant numbers of students from Britain's Asian minorities. Another major change to working conditions was the provision of desk top computers, a resource of great benefit to the production of teaching materials in spite of the inordinate amounts of time that some of those particularly fascinated by the possibilities of the new technology initially devoted to customizing one-off adaptations for their own use.

Throughout the period a shift had been taking place in the profile of the Department of Phonetics and Linguistics, with the centre of gravity moving from phonetics and descriptive linguistics of a kind clearly related and relevant to the language studies being practised in the regional departments towards a more theoretical stance more naturally aligned with philosophy and psychology. While the intellectual distinction of its leading members was unquestioned, student numbers were not especially high, and there was therefore in some quarters an increased querying of the place of the Department within SOAS.

These trends formed the background to the stormy events of 1992, which were certainly some of the most dramatic in the School's recent history. SOAS was threatened by yet another major funding crisis, provoked this time by failure to secure from the University Funding Council any guarantee of the continuation of the special factor funding on which SOAS had for so long been massively dependent. Severe cuts had to be contemplated, and at an overnight meeting away from the School the management team reached the conclusion that the least damaging way of achieving these would be through closure of the Department of Phonetics and Linguistics at the end of the academic session, with virtually immediate effect.

On 27 May this proposal was put to the Heads of Departments Committee, which recommended its rejection to the scheduled meeting of Academic Board which immediately followed on that same day. A stormy debate followed, at which all the predictable arguments were strongly advanced against the most forceful of the School's recent Directors in favour of the need for further consideration before undertaking such a radical step, involving the excision of one of the School's outstanding research departments. It was agreed that the matter should be held over to an extraordinary meeting of Academic Board. In the meantime the powerful networking capacity of the department was activated and, in a quite exceptional demonstration of international academic organization, the Director's office was inundated by expressions of grave concern about the threat to this historic department from leading figures in phonetics and linguistics across the world. The extraordinary meeting of Academic Board on 9 June was unswayed by Michael McWilliam's spirited defence of the management's decision, and it was resolved that other means should be found to cope with the large impending deficit.

This was remitted to a senior working party, chaired by David Parkin, which scratched around in the usual fashion for savings. Most of these, it has to be said, were irritatingly symbolic rather than substantially effective, like the recommendation that tea and biscuits should no longer be served at committee meetings, no matter how protracted their agendas. But this working party achieved a rather larger place in the history of the School when it was given the task of liasing with the committee chaired by John Raisman which had been set up to make recommendations to the Funding Council on the case for continuation of the School's non-formula funding.

A great deal of work went into the preparation of a reasoned case for special support of the distinctive but expensive remit inherent in the School's specialist mission for Asian and African studies. This was the first time for a generation that this had had to be done, and much time was spent elaborating the picture of the intimate relationship between all the School's activities and the special place of languages within those. Searching questions were asked by the Raisman committee on its several visits to the School, particularly by its academic members, Professor Richard Bowring from Cambridge and Dr Richard Werbner from Manchester, who needed careful convincing that SOAS was no longer making the prodigal use of over-generous resources of which it could rightly have been accused twenty years earlier. At one point in November 1992, we felt forced to draw up an internal list of languages that would progressively have to be sacrificed, depending on the cuts to the level of support hitherto received which seemed all too likely. The future of SOAS language studies had never looked bleaker.

Act III: Reconstruction and revival

Gonca gibi hâr-ı gamdan yüregüm pür-hûn iken
Gülbün ü gülzâr-ı bahtum verdi berg ü bâr gül

My grief-pierced heart turned crimson like the bud
but now my fortune's garden blossoms like the rose

Hayâlî

In the event, however, the hard work which had gone into the School's defence paid off, and early in 1993 the Funding Council largely accepted the case that had been put, thus permitting SOAS language studies not only to continue with some reasonable future security, but also to develop in new directions. The changes that have taken place over the last ten years are largely the product of ideas adumbrated during the previous decade. The difference has been that the pace of change has gathered, and much that was previously talked about has started to be seriously implemented.

Changes were certainly needed, if language studies were to take their full place in the new SOAS, an institution which was being transformed by the rapid increase in student numbers which was required if the School were to survive in the new conditions of British higher education. By this time, most of those involved with language studies had over the past ten years increasingly felt their subjects to be unappreciated and under threat, as resources were increasingly given to other parts of SOAS, especially law and the social sciences, which were palpably expanding at a rapid rate while languages at best stood still. These feelings were reciprocated by a sense elsewhere that, as most departments' staff-student ratios steadily rose, so small a portion of the ever increasing burden was falling on the language teachers. Although such thinking did not always take into account the special conditions imposed by language teaching, with its need for smaller groups and higher class-contact hours, this view certainly did not lack justification. In other areas, too, the language side could be seen not to be quite pulling its proper weight, as in the 1992 Research Assessment Exercise, when the excellent 5 grade awarded to Phonetics and Linguistics was not matched by the regional departments, which received only 4s in the Asian Studies and Middle Eastern and African Studies units of assessment.

In the post-Raisman era, there was therefore much to be done to ensure the future vitality of language studies. While the subsequent story of the last few years has had its share of downs and ups, it is remarkable how much has been achieved, partly as the result of successful adaptation to change, partly as the result of implementing ideas which had earlier only been discussed.

Teaching performance has now rightly become a major criterion of success for British university departments. Greatly increased travel opportunities mean that many British students today, unlike those of an earlier period, come with some first hand experience of Asia and Africa. The numbers of students for the major languages, Chinese, Japanese and Arabic have now become very significant, and there have been noteworthy increases in the numbers studying languages of the next tier, such as Indonesian, Hindi, or Swahili. At the same time more careful provision has been made for the language needs of Masters students. In keeping with the general trend of students in all language departments throughout the British system, the strongest demand is for an emphasis on practical language skills rather than the intensive study of literary texts. To meet this demand, the quality of all these language programmes has been much strengthened by progressive modernization of teaching materials, the establishment of year abroad language study programmes, and by the appointment of increased numbers of professional language lectors to the staff of the regional departments. External teaching quality audits of the regional departments in the late 1990s confirmed their very high standard of performance with near-maximum scores of 22 and 23 out of 24.

Meanwhile, the needs of non-degree students, including the important constituency of government and business for which SOAS has from its inception been rightly seen to have a special responsibility, have been catered for by significant administrative changes. In 1996 a Language Centre was created from the former External Services Division, and has proved extremely successful in delivering high-quality teaching to a great variety of students under the academic supervision of the language departments. The scale of the Language Centre's operations rises annually, and not only includes teaching across the whole geographical range of the School's remit but also offers courses in a good many Asian and African languages which cannot be covered by the departments themselves.

The more realistic and outgoing attitudes towards making the School's language expertise more widely available have their parallel in the keener awareness in the regional departments of the need for a much more actively organized research culture than was the case in the comfortable past. This has been partly the product of the successive Research Assessment Exercises. It has also partly been the product of the changed internal composition of the regional departments, where the exodus of specialists in other arts and humanities subjects has led to there being a greater proportion of literature specialists. This resource was first capitalized upon with the establishment of a cross-departmental MA in Comparative Literature (Africa/Asia) in 1993. The experience of shared teaching on this programme led in 1995 to the establishment of a Panel for Comparative Literature in 1995, which encouraged a number of workshops and discussion groups which were beginning to pay some serious attention to issues raised by critical theory and contemporary criticism. These approaches had been rather neglected in the departments but were making a significant entrance into the School's intellectual life with the appointment of critically aware members of staff with responsibilities for teaching Asian and African English-language literature, itself a particularly attractive field for postgraduate students.

The unique possibilities which SOAS provides for comparative literary work were splendidly realized in the memorable conference on the Qasida in Asia and Africa organized by Stefan Sperl in 1994, at which panels of international specialists, including members of four of the School's regional departments, explored the ramifications of the prime genre of classical Arabic poetry across the huge spread of later Islamic literatures from Hausa to Indonesian. The substantial proceedings are recorded in *Qasida Poetry in Islamic Asia and Africa* (1996), one of whose volumes contains bilingual texts of 50 qasidas in 14 languages, including the one in Ottoman Turkish from which the epigraph to this section is taken.

Numerous other strands have started to emerge in the research interests of staff of the regional departments, including both new developments and expansions of well-established activities. Film studies and cultural studies might be cited as examples of the first, while a case of the second would be the continuing special contribution of SOAS scholars to the textual study of religions, which is pursued both in the Department of the Study of Religions and in the Departments of Languages and Cultures. In the case of Islam, a particular direction to such studies was given by the establishment in 1995 thanks to a generous Saudi Arabian endowment of the King Fahd Chair of Islamic Studies, first held by Muhammad Abdel Haleem.

Meanwhile, the traditional strengths of SOAS in the description of Asian and African languages have continued to be reflected in a steady stream of publications. The increased commitment to language teaching and to making Asian and African languages accessible to a wider public is reflected in the numbers of standard teaching grammars compiled by members of staff of the regional departments. Others are engaged in primary research on these languages, as they have been from the School's earliest days. It may be noted that, with five out of the seven SOAS Fellows of the British Academy, the regional departments had the same number and proportion in 2002 as they had had in 1966. Two have produced recent work of outstanding significance on ancient languages, David Hawkins in the definitive primary study of Hieroglyphic Luwian and Nicholas Sims-Williams on Bactrian and other Iranian languages. On the modern side, Dick Hayward has produced notable studies of the Omotic and Cushitic languages of East Africa, while George Hewitt has worked on Georgian and Abkhaz and Christopher Shackle on Siraiki and Panjabi.

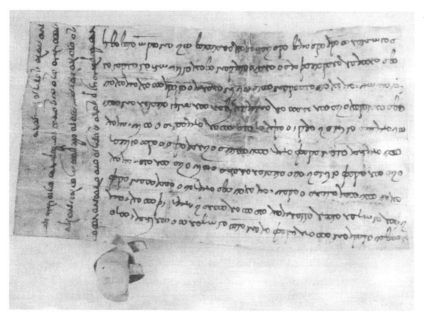

A Bactrian letter

If the linguists have thus continued to thrive, the linguisticians have had a harder time, as painful changes have been experienced by the Department of Phonetics and Linguistics. Although the attempt made in 1992 to close down the department had been foiled, an increased emphasis on theoretical linguistics under the outstanding intellectual leadership of Ruth Kempson (herself a Fellow of the British Academy) continued to cause difficulties in perceptions of its fit with the rest of the School. The widening gulf might be symbolized by the puzzled reaction of most SOAS members of the audience at what is generally remembered as the most impenetrable of all recent professorial inaugural lectures, that on 'Semantic Types for Natural Languages' given by Shalom Lappin in February 1997. By that time several members of the department (which lost Phonetics from its title) had transferred to regional departments, and when Kempson and Lappin themselves both left for King's College in 1998 at yet another time of financial stringency, the decision was taken not to fill their posts. The further shrinkage of the department with the departure of Jonathan Kaye in 1999 after a brief and troubled period as its head necessitated a re-design of the Department's reduced role and teaching portfolio.

With the turn of the millennium, however, the beginnings of a whole new chapter in the chequered story of SOAS language-studies were established by a series of external and internal developments. First, the long-delayed review of the School's non-formula funding was eventually conducted in 2000 as a special exercise within the HEFCE scheme of funding for Minority Subjects. A report from the School carefully reinforced the case for the continuation of the funding made available since the Raisman award of 1993. The result was a substantial success, with the preservation for at least a further five years of the School's special funding for most of the Asian and African languages taught in the regional departments, as minority subjects.

In the same year, the new prominence which literary studies have assumed at SOAS was recognized by the award by the Arts and Humanities Research Board of a large five-year grant to support a Centre for Asian and African Literatures at SOAS in collaboration with University College. Building upon the earlier initiatives of the Comparative Literature Panel, the successful bid was led by Drew Gerstle. He is now Director of the Centre, which is running several major research projects pulling together the literature specialists across the School's regions and enabling them to work with circles of distinguished international scholars. This success certainly played its part in the improved rating for the regional departments in the 2001 Research Assessment Exercise. After their disappointing run of 4s in 1992 and 1996, they were at last awarded the 5s needed both for some future financial security and in order to retain full academic credibility within the British university system.

Like all departments in that system, the SOAS language departments have suffered the strains that go with trying to do more with fewer resources while also being subject to continual external account. In the case of the smaller departments, the number of potential office holders was becoming exhausted, and in 1998 the Departments of South Asia and South East Asia were administratively joined, rather like England and Scotland in the Stuart period, under a single Head with a single departmental office. With the arrival of Colin Bundy as Director, the long overdue opportunity was taken to overhaul the School's academic organization, and a Working Party was established in October 2001. As the result of its recommendations, a new Faculty of Languages and Cultures was established in August 2002, headed as Dean by Graham Furniss who in an earlier incarnation had been responsible for the creation of the Language Centre. Made up of the five regional departments, the Department of Linguistics and the Language Centre, the new Faculty should allow programmes of both teaching and research to be planned and administered in a more effective and rational way than the fragmented previous system always permitted.

It seemed as if the Department of Linguistics might only be able to play a very minor role in the new scheme of things. But after the reductions and discouragements it has suffered in recent years, its fortunes were suddenly reversed in the summer of 2002 by an unexpected and munificent award from the Lisbet Rausing Charitable Fund for a research and documentation programme for endangered languages. Besides a ten-year world research programme administered by the School, new posts are being created within SOAS which will greatly strengthen both the Department of Linguistics and the new Centre for Language Research which is designed to bring together the School's language specialists in a similar way to that performed for literary scholars by the AHRB Centre. The Hans Rausing Endangered Languages Project will be directed by Peter Austin, recently appointed as Märit Rausing Professor of Field Linguistics.

All these recent developments are hugely encouraging for all those who are involved with language studies at SOAS. No British university can expect a return to the comfortable circumstances of the good old days, which the SOAS language departments once enjoyed in such very special measure. With the typical change in atmosphere from club to office, there are now substantially fewer specialists in Asian and African languages at the School than there were thirty years ago, but there has equally been a substantial rise in all-round professionalism amongst the notably international body of serving members of staff in the six departments which are now constituent members of the Faculty of Languages and Cultures. The leaner and hungrier lives of the contemporary academic world do require hope for their sustenance, above all the hope of having opportunities to do a better and more interesting job. And after too many brushes with despair, it is this precious gift which has been restored by substantial recent encouragements to what will always be a defining activity of the SOAS mission.

5

The arts and humanities: Between history and ethnography

J. D. Y. Peel

Methods of enquiry

The Departments of History and of Anthropology and Sociology are the principal custodians of two of the fundamental methods of enquiry that are used widely across the whole School: the recovery of the past through the analysis of its documentary and material traces, and ethnography, which derives accounts of other cultures through personal engagement with their members. They are variably employed, for the former is predominant in relation to the remoter past, while the latter is more relevant to the recent past which reaches into the present. As methods they call for different kinds of expertise, which to a large extent define mastery of the two disciplines, so they generate a degree of rivalry; but in practice they are interdependent, since usually an element of each is required in any enquiry into any society or culture, past or present. For while the roots of the present lie in the past, the past is also the object of continuous re-evaluation as an essential aspect of social action in the present.

The other departments treated in this chapter – Art and Archaeology, the Study of Religions, and Music – also employ these two methods. The proportions in which they do so vary according to both period (the earlier being the more dependent on documentary sources, while the recent tend to be more ethnographic), and region (ethnographic approaches being more salient in the study of Africa than on the ancient literate cultures of Asia). The importance of ethnomusicology, with its orientation to real-life practice in contemporary non-Western musical traditions, also derives from the fact that, uniquely to the Music Department, performance plays a key role in both research and teaching. In these more cultural disciplines a third method also comes prominently into play: the analysis of texts, art objects and musical items in terms of their intrinsic qualities, such as their form and symbolic content, the principles of their composition and so forth. This third approach, of course, is primary in the work of the regional or 'language and culture' departments; and this serves to remind us that there is no sharp distinction between it and the work of the so-called 'humanities' departments treated in this chapter. Just as several members of the regional departments have qualifications in anthropology or pursue lines of inquiry that are history pure and simple, so the creation of new departments for art, religion and music from the late 1980s came about largely by transferring staff who had been well at home in the regional departments.

Much blurring and overlap are also to be found on the other side, where the humanities march with the social sciences. Here a fourth basic method comes into play: formal model-building to test theories against empirical data, quantified where possible. While this method has its main field of application in economics, it also has a vital role to play in economic history and even has its uses in anthropology. Conversely, in so far as the School's social scientists work principally on current developments, and that in a way which involves much first-hand interpretation of contemporary data (such as government statistics or the 'grey literature' of development agencies or interviews with local political figures), their approach has to be far more ethnographic than that of most social scientists; and what most members of the Department of Political Studies actually write is high-quality contemporary history. These five 'humanities' departments, then, do not in themselves form a discrete grouping, a natural class, but the central segment of a broad spectrum of intellectual endeavour, with many affinities and cross-connections linking them with other work across the whole School. It is a characteristic dilemma of SOAS academics in general that they have to negotiate for themselves a balance between the demands of region and of discipline. The departments treated here vary considerably both in how they do this and in the relative weight they place on either component, with History tending to lay most stress on region and Anthropology more on disciplinary or thematic focus, and the others at various points in between.

History

The Department of History was one of the original departments of the School. By the late 1960s it had become the largest and was perhaps the most distinguished, whether judged by the eminence of its senior professors or by the number of PhD theses it produced. For a decade these averaged over 18 a year and comprised not far short of 40 percent of the School's total. At its zenith in 1974, it had 35 full-time members of staff: 7 professors, 7 readers and 21 lecturers, with a coverage in depth of all SOAS's regions. Not surprisingly, it was the most 'ex-colonial' regions – South Asia and Africa – which (at 9 apiece) then had the most generous provision, and between them accounted for roughly two-thirds of all History PhD theses in the boom years from the late 1960s into the early 1980s. But such generous staffing levels were not to be maintained, and by the early 1990s, History was accorded a staff establishment of 21.

Of all the disciplines considered here, history in general is least concerned to openly articulate the theories and methods which inform its practice. One learns how to be a historian, less through an introductory course on historical methods, than in one's third year, when the historian's craft is communicated through an intense study of the documents relevant to a particular 'special subject'. The corollary of this is the importance of region: to the cliché that historians defend themselves with the protestation 'not my period', the SOAS historian might well add 'not my region'. Apart from posts in economic history (where the quotient of theory and comparison is higher), region is crosscut mainly by period, with some posts designated for the 'ancient' or for the 'contemporary' or 'modern' history of the region. Malcolm Yapp, himself a historian of the modern Middle East, commented in his 1982 Report on the School's organization that trans-regional courses were of secondary importance, though there were some posts which bridged regions: East and South East Asia or Africa and the Middle East. So the historians (unlike, say, the anthropologists) are informally divided into regional 'sections' within the department, and history degrees used to be divided into various regional 'branches', or were designated by their predominant region of study (even though a broader 'Modern Third World' option was also available). The move from the old University-wide syllabus to the SOAS-based course-unit system in the late 1970s led to a large increase in students taking history courses in joint degrees or as 'floaters'.

For close on thirty years up to the late 1980s, the History Department was headed by only three men: Bernard Lewis (1957-74), W.G. Beasley (1974-78) and Roland Oliver (1978-86), historians respectively of the Middle East, Japan and Africa. They all belonged to that age-cohort which had seen war service. Lewis (who had joined the staff of the School in 1938) served first in the Royal Armoured Corps and then in Intelligence in the Middle East. Beasley did his in the Royal Navy Volunteer Reserve and Oliver had worked at Bletchley Park, both joining the School after the War. A comparison of their achievements sheds much light on the different challenges and opportunities presented by their various regions. Lewis wrote across the whole range of Middle Eastern history from the rise of Islam onwards: his first book on the origins of Ismailism, his much reprinted *The Arabs in History* (1959), then books on topics as diverse as the origins of modern Turkey, the Ottoman Empire, two volumes on early-to-medieval Islam, a monograph on the Assassins, several works on the mutual perceptions of Islam and Europe. Beasley's *oeuvre* was almost as masterly but more compact: starting from a study of Anglo-Japanese relations in the nineteenth century, he wrote two authoritative histories of modern Japan (1963 and 1990), separated by books on the Meiji restoration (1972) and on twentieth-century Japanese imperialism (1987). Oliver's achievement was quite different again, since African history did not exist as a field of study when in 1948 he was first appointed lecturer in the 'tribal history of East Africa'. He not only established African History at SOAS, but was also one of a handful of scholars who defined the subject as it is known today worldwide.

By tradition, however, the 'senior section' of the department was South Asia. At the start of this period, C. H. Philips was still Professor of Oriental History: he had written an important book on the East India Company and kept his historian's hand in after he became Director. The Department drew many research students from South Asia itself, who went on to staff history departments at home, and two (B. N. Pandey and Z. H. Zaidi) joined the SOAS staff. The historiography of South Asia was deeply shaped by the long British presence in India – the India Office Library continues to be the most widely used resource for its historians – even though the post-1947 research agenda dictated a move beyond imperial history to the study of indigenous forces and pre-colonial currents, nationalism and its aftermath, 'subaltern studies' and so forth. After Philips's elevation, the leading active Indianist was K. A. Ballhatchet, who dealt with the period of the Raj, but with its social and cultural aspects: education, social policy, missions, sex and race, caste and class. In economic history there was K. N. Chaudhuri, whose work culminated in studies of the interplay of trade and civilization in the Indian Ocean of Braudelian scope. From Peter Hardy on the Mughal Empire to Avril Powell on religious encounters at a later period Islamic North India got extensive treatment. The lecturers in the 'ancient history of South Asia' – Wendy Doniger O'Flaherty, succeeded in 1975 by A. Piatigorsky – were in effect scholars of Hindu myth and philosophy. During the early 1990s, after Ballhatchet had retired and Chaudhuri moved on, a new leadership came to the fore. Peter Robb's studies of political and agrarian topics led up to what is perhaps the supreme test of a mature SOAS historian, a large-scale, long-span history of a region, in his *A History of India* (2002); while David Arnold, closely linked with the Subaltern Studies group, wrote extensively on the empire in relation to famine, environment, medicine and the body.

The historiographic overhang of the British Empire affects South East Asia to a lesser extent than it does India. Yet still this was where it began: the first professor, C. D. Cowan (who succeeded Philips as Director in 1976), was a historian of British activity in nineteenth-century Malaya. But what is remarkable about the South East Asia section of the department during the rapid growth of the 1950s and 1960s, is how far its coverage went beyond this, with work on Indonesia by J. G. de Casparis and Merle Ricklefs grounded in Dutch *Indologie* and the traditions of indigenous Java. In contrast to these stood Malcolm Caldwell, lecturer in the economic history of East as well as South East Asia, whose Marxist critique of imperialism and underdevelopment ran from Indonesia to China; and Ralph Smith, whose massive *International History of the Vietnam War* appeared in three volumes between 1984 and 1991. In fact, South East Asia was much more generously provided for than the stringency of the times could allow, and no section of the Department had to endure such a shrinkage through the 1980s: from six posts in 1974 to just one in 2001. This was the economic historian Ian Brown, whose work covered the whole mainland region, latterly with a particular focus on Burma.

As an historical field, East Asia offers some striking, even paradoxical contrasts. Its major constituents, China and Japan, having more or less avoided European colonialism, demand a different periodization and their knowable history long predates contact with the West. To work from primary sources their historians need to possess exceptionally demanding language skills, which reduces the pool of research students and can draw staff away. So at the department's apogee in the early 1970s, compared with the other sections, the level of East Asia's staffing was not commensurate with its size and importance, though Richard Sims worked long-term on political and diplomatic history, while for a decade economic history was covered by Kaoru Sugihara. China never had a Beasley, and the most promising sinologist of the early 1970s, Endymion Wilkinson, left for a career outside the academy. The coverage of China had to be completely reconstructed in the late 1980s, and with the appointment of T. H. (Tim) Barrett – whose primary interest was religion and the state in medieval China – to a chair of East Asian History in 1986, Chinese history took a much more cultural turn. Frank Dikötter's work on Chinese medicine and ideology consolidated this trend. With Martina Deuchler on Korean history, the coverage of East Asia in the 1990s was stronger than it had been for several decades.

91

As far as the History Department is concerned, the history of the Middle East begins with the rise of Islam, for its ancient history – Anatolia, Persia, Mesopotamia chiefly – has by convention belonged to the Near and Middle East Department. After Lewis's departure, the leading professor in the section was P. M. Holt, whose interests ranged from Mamluk Egypt to nineteenth-century Sudan. In economic history there was Michael Cook, whose original research had been on medieval Anatolia, but who also worked on early Islam. The leading figure for the modern period was M. E. Yapp, essentially a political and diplomatic historian, whose work had shifted from India and Afghanistan to the Middle East. A sequence of appointments in the 1970s gave better coverage to the more outlying and non-Arab regions: Michael Brett for the Maghreb, Colin Heywood for Ottoman history and David Morgan for medieval Persia and the Mongols. But the most novel development did not originate in History but in the Near and Middle East Department, namely the radical approach to the origins of Islam put forward by John Wansbrough, which challenged the 'internalist' orthodoxy and proposed that Islam had developed within a much wider 'sectarian milieu'. This controversial view – which meant, in effect, treating the history of early Islam along lines long applied to early Christianity – found its home among historians rather than Koranic specialists. It underlay later work by Cook and by Gerald Hawting, whose own subject was precisely the traditions of early Islam. By the late 1990s, only Brett and Hawting remained from the 1970s and younger scholars were coming in, with (as in South Asia) a certain shift to more cultural topics such as gender, ideology and education.

Finally Africa, where (more than for any other regional section) the collective achievement of SOAS historians was greater than the sum of their individual works. Up to 1961 there were only three members of staff and there was no BA degree specializing in African history. So Roland Oliver was able to concentrate on defining the subject and setting a research agenda. He himself wrote respected books on missionaries and on imperialism in nineteenth-century Africa, but saw that the real challenge was to push the horizon of African history back in time though such means as the analysis of oral tradition – where the anthropologists were often discouraging – archaeology and historical linguistics. He travelled extensively in Africa across what was largely an academic *terra incognita*, and placed SOAS at the centre of the emerging network of African historians. He set up the African History Seminar in 1952, and convened international conferences on African History and Archaeology at SOAS in 1953 and 1957. There began that stream of research students – a flood by the early 1960s, including many Africans – who would go on to fill so many of the newly created posts in African History throughout the world, whether in African universities or elsewhere. Oliver's key collaborator was J. D. Fage (at SOAS 1959-62), with whom in 1960 he started the *Journal of African History*, wrote the standard *Short History of Africa* (1962), and edited the *Cambridge History of Africa* (8 volumes, 1975-86), which showed authoritatively that the subject now existed. Oliver's chair came at last in 1964.

In 1961 another round of expansion began, first with the appointment of Richard Gray, who had written books on Rhodesia and the Sudan, and had an abiding interest in Christian missions. Others followed to create a systematic coverage of the continent: Humphrey Fisher on African Islam, David Birmingham on Portuguese trade and empire, Andrew Roberts on the pre-colonial history of Central and East Africa and Richard Rathbone on modern West Africa, with a focus on political change in Ghana. Of this wave, the most eminent was Shula Marks, who not only pioneered new approaches in the social history of South Africa – especially on the subject of gender – but through her many research students and good connections inside South Africa played a fundamental role in shaping its historiography during the difficult later years of apartheid. In 1995 she followed Lewis, Beasley, Holt, Chaudhuri and Oliver to election as a Fellow of the British Academy. Somewhat later came the economic historian W.G. Clarence-Smith, whose early work had been on Angola, but by the 1990s had become the most serious comparativist in the Department, with work on cocoa in three continents and on the commercial system of the Indian Ocean. The end of that decade brought a wave of fresh appointments mostly to re-fill some of the slots vacated by retirements, particularly in South and West Africa, and in African Islam.

History remains one of the key departments in the School: not just large and diverse, but a point of reference for the many members of other departments who pursue historical lines of inquiry, particularly in the language departments, Anthropology and Politics. It does not promote a distinct type of historiography (beyond the focus on Asia and Africa), though a certain shift to more cultural and social topics is evident among the younger staff, in accordance with general trends in the discipline. There has also been a shift towards the modern period, which is manifestly more relevant to contemporary concerns, but runs the risk of neglecting those older, indigenous springs of history outside Europe which SOAS historians are uniquely called to address. For in a profession dominated by historians of Britain, Europe and North America, and a world where the weight of population shifts steadily from North to South and West to East, SOAS's regionalist mission is more important than ever. Still, the 5* grades which History gained in the Research Assessment Exercises of 1996 and 2001 showed that its members' efforts did go not unappreciated by their peers.

Anthropology and Sociology

The Department of Cultural Anthropology (as it was first styled) was founded in 1949, in the post-war climate of expanded opportunity for the subject signalized by the establishment of the Colonial Social Science Research Council. It was also a time when the distinctively British tradition of social anthropology, with its commitment to intense fieldwork and its theoretical paradigm of 'structural-functionalism', was reaching its apogee. Yet the man who headed the new department for a quarter of a century, Christoph von Fürer-Haimendorf, stood somewhat apart from his compeers who took over the other main anthropology departments at about this time. For though he had attended Bronislaw Malinowski's famous seminar at LSE in 1935-36, he remained fundamentally attached to the German ethnological tradition in which he had been formed at the University of Vienna. In a curious reprise of anthropology's history, Fürer-Haimendorf had been on his way to a further spell of fieldwork on the Nagas in northeast India when, just like Malinowski during the First World War, he was first interned as an enemy alien; but thanks to his excellent relations with colonial officials, he was merely confined to Hyderabad State, where he was able to conduct research on the Nizam's tribal subjects. After the war, he did extensive fieldwork in a third region of the subcontinent, Nepal, so initiating the School's reputation as the prime British centre for the ethnography of South Asia. Fürer-Haimendorf was not just highly prolific – he wrote in all over twenty books – but pioneered the use of photographs and film in ethnography.

Fürer-Haimendorf ran the department in a gentlemanly way, being concerned to appoint staff for their personal as well as their intellectual qualities, and certainly SOAS got the reputation of having one of the most friendly and harmonious anthropology departments. As fresh appointments were made to cover all the major regions of Asia and Africa – at first necessarily of people trained in other universities – the theoretical cast of the department moved towards the British mainstream, a shift completed under the next Head of Department (1976-84), another Indianist, Adrian Mayer. Mayer also led the way forward from rather static tribal or village studies when he followed up his classic monograph on a village in Madhya Pradesh with one on Indian peasants in Fiji. Still, the regional identification of SOAS anthropologists remained much stronger than elsewhere. To this day, research supervisors are primarily chosen on the basis of region, and the availability of seven regional ethnography courses – Middle East, South Asia, South East Asia, China, Japan, East and West Africa – is a proudly maintained feature of both the BA and the MA degrees taught in the department. On the other hand, regional identity has never been as strong in Anthropology as in History, and has always been expected to be complemented by particular thematic or theoretical interests. By the 1990s regionalism came under further pressure: partly from the Research Assessment Exercise (RAE), which entailed direct comparison with other anthropology departments without specific regional commitments, thus tending to elevate general or theoretical criteria; and partly from the growth of specialist MA courses which prioritized thematic over regional expertise.

In 1961, with the general expansion of the social sciences throughout the School, the Department had been renamed 'of Anthropology and Sociology', with the latter mainly represented by R. P. Dore, who held a chair in the sociology of Japan, jointly with LSE. When he left, sociology as such fell into abeyance, though appointments might still be made from those with a sociological, rather than anthropological, background. By 1967, the department had expanded to 13 members of staff, a level which it would roughly maintain for the next twenty years. South Asia continued to be a primary focus of SOAS ethnography, with Lionel Caplan beginning a series of studies of politics, social change and religion that would stretch from Nepal to Madras. Next came Africa, with the problems posed by its newly independent countries strongly shaping the research agenda. East Africa was represented at professorial level by Philip Gulliver, who was replaced in 1972 by John Middleton, while among junior staff David Parkin and Paul Spencer started to build up their reputations at SOAS. For West Africa there was Abner Cohen, whose earlier work had been on the Middle East. The Middle East and South East Asia were each served by young lecturers who would spend their whole careers at the School: Richard Tapper and Andrew Turton. East Asia was more problematic: it had not been a classic region of anthropological research and for a number of years it proved hard to maintain continuity in its coverage. Stephan Feuchtwang, the Department's first China specialist, was one of a handful of staff across the School whose appointments were terminated in 1973 because of their active sympathy with student protest. Thereafter, Japan and China each had a single post. It was not till the 1990s that East Asia was solidly established, in terms of both staff supply and student demand.

In the 1960s the dominant theoretical stance of the Department was 'action theory', one of the main alternatives to structural-functionalism. Its focus on individual actors was challenged by Abner Cohen who set out his position in a run of significant books – notably *Custom and Politics in Urban Africa* (1969) and *Two-Dimensional Man* (1974) – which established him as the main intellectual pivot of the Department during the 1970s. Cohen's focus on ethnicity and urbanism expressed the subject's move away from 'tribal' and village studies, as it adjusted itself to new historical realities. Parkin's studies of urban ethnicity in East Africa addressed similar themes, while his little monograph on economic aspects of Islamic conversion was even more directly influenced by Cohen's work on the relationship between power and the symbolic order. During the 1980s a group of colleagues around David Parkin extended this focus towards a fuller analysis of semantics and epistemology, linking it in the process to Michel Foucault's theory of power, then much in the ascendant. (Perhaps this was manifest destiny, since the School's motto, 'Knowledge Is Power' encapsulates a great deal of Foucault's message.) Parkin edited two influential volumes of essays: *Semantic Anthropology* (1983) and *The Anthropology of Evil* (1985) on these themes. Contributors to them included such other SOAS anthropologists as Mark Hobart (who in a trenchant series of articles drew on his Balinese ethnography to mount a penetrating critique of much anthropological writing), and Brian Moeran, whose interests focused on Japanese 'cultural work', from craft pottery to advertising. While much solidly *social* anthropological work continued to be done – for example, by Tapper on nomads and the state in Iran, by Spencer on the structure of East African pastoralists, and by Turton on the Thai peasantry – there is no doubt that there was a definite shift towards more *cultural* topics and to a greater concern with theory. This led in the late 1980s to a marked shift in the focus of the undergraduate syllabus, as the old institutional approach known as PERKS (Politics, Economics, Religion, Kinship, Symbolism) was replaced by one based on a strong theoretical core running through the three years. In fact, the SOAS department did much to set the trend by which anthropology departments in Britain shifted towards a more reflexive, 'post-modernist' conception of the subject.

The late 1980s brought major changes of personnel. With the retirement of the most senior figures, Parkin was for a while the only professor, as well as Head of Department (1984-87). The void in the coverage of West Africa that followed Cohen's departure was filled by the appointment of Richard Fardon in 1988 and of J. D. Y. Peel in 1989. Both were specialists of Nigeria and shared interests in the anthropology/history interface, religion, comparative studies, and the history of the social sciences. A new specialism, in the anthropology of development, began to crystallize with the arrival (both originally as research fellows) of Elisabeth Croll, who published an impressive sequence of sociological studies on gender and development in China, and of Johan Pottier, who worked on Central Africa with a particular interest in the provision of food. As student numbers rose from the late 1980s, fresh appointments were made to produce a variety of new combinations of region and theme: China/education, Japan/tourism, Middle East/gender, Central Africa/medical anthropology, West Africa/ecology and development. By the late 1990s, Lola Martinez (for Japan) and Kit Davis (for medical anthropology) were in the greatest demand as research supervisors. To a growing extent, patterns of student demand, both for the burgeoning MA courses and for MPhil/PhD topics, shaped the specification of new posts. In the mid-1990s there emerged spontaneously across the whole School a nexus of people with an interest in media studies, but most of the intellectual drive came from Anthropology, where two further media appointments were made, respectively in South India and China. It was now a lesser priority to cover all 'traditional' regions than to ensure that there was adequate staffing in the key thematic specialisms. At the same time there remained a strong sense of the importance of the theoretical 'mainstream', and a good generic competence was expected of all new appointees.

In its early years, the department had had no undergraduates at all, and it was not until the mid-1970s that they reached over a dozen a year, and then they were all joint-subject students. The view was expressly taken that, since single-subject anthropology degrees were offered at other London colleges, SOAS should offer a more specialized product, of anthropology combined with subjects not available elsewhere. This might be a language, linguistics, or (most often) history, particularly African or South Asian. The first single-subject anthropology students – nine of them – graduated in 1981. Anthropology's contribution to MA teaching was at first mostly through ethnography courses taken as part of the MA in Area Studies, but in 1984 an MA in Social Anthropology was introduced. While for a minority this served either as a 'conversion course' for students who had taken some other subject for their first degree but wanted to do research in anthropology, for most it was a 'one-off', taken for professional advancement, to mark a change in life-course or simply for the intellectual interest. During the 1990s there was a dramatic rise in MA numbers, particularly when three specialist MAs – Development, Medical and later Media – were added to the original generic course, thus making the SOAS department the national 'market leader' in MA courses in anthropology.

SOAS Anthropology gained a Grade 5 in three successive RAEs, and its senior members played prominent roles in the discipline. Parkin chaired the Association of Social Anthropologists for 1989-1993, and Fardon did so from 2001. Peel was elected a Fellow of the British Academy in 1991, and Parkin in 1993. Peel won the Herskovits Award of the African Studies Association in the US for his *Religious Encounter and the Making of the Yoruba* (2000). But what the Department prided itself upon was its all-round strength and cohesiveness. No small part was played in this by some excellent department secretaries and by Helen Kanitkar. Originally appointed by Fürer-Haimendorf to work on the Bibliography of South Asia, Helen's main role was to run the small Departmental Library, a great boon to students and a strong focus of collective identity. She was appreciated alike for the lucidity of her first-year classes and the kindly counsel she gave to generations of students. Her sudden death early in 2002 broke the last direct link with the days of Fürer-Haimendorf. The Departmental Library is now named in her memory.

Art and Archaeology

This was the first of the three cultural disciplines which since 1990 have been hived off from the regional departments to become independent entities. When its forerunner, the Centre for Art and Archaeology, was created in 1981, seventeen members of staff were associated with it, of whom six held posts that included reference to art and/or archaeology in the title. Their regional connections were strongly skewed towards East Asia and the Middle East. For the former there was the incomparable resource of the Percival David Foundation of Chinese Art, which also sponsored periodic international colloquia on Asian art. The Foundation had long been headed by William Watson, who held a chair dedicated to the art and archaeology of China, and published with distinction across the whole field. East Asia claimed two other posts (including a research officer for the Buddhist Art Project), while the Departments of South Asia and South East Asia each had a single post. The Near and Middle East Department had two highly research-active staff (both eventually promoted to personal chairs) in A.D.H. Bivar and G. Fehérvári. Though they sometimes published together, Bivar was more the archaeologist, working for most of his career on the site of Ghubayra in southeast Iran, which spanned the Sassanid and Islamic periods; while Fehérvári focused on Islamic arts, especially pottery and metalwork. During the 1970s and 1980s, the Islamic world claimed more research degrees than any other region, followed by China. Africa had no post to itself until John Picton was appointed as lecturer in African art in 1979.

The move from Centre to Department took place in 1990, amid extensive changes on all fronts. Having chaired the Centre since 1986, Picton remained steady at the helm, with a dozen full-time teaching staff (some with duties in other departments). Within a few years there were many staff replacements. Roderick Whitfield had already taken over from Watson as Head of the Percival David Foundation and Professor of Chinese and East Asian Art. Philip Denwood continued with his long-term studies of Tibetan architecture, while further appointments on Korea, Japan, and China consolidated the strong coverage of East Asia. In 1999 an arrangement made through the Sainsbury Institute for the Study of Japanese Arts and Culture, a joint venture between the SOAS Department and the University of East Anglia, permitted a further Japanese post.

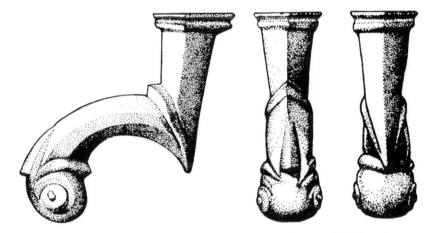

Bronze objects from Ghubayra

The important Islamic area received a great fillip from the endowment in 1990 of a new chair of Islamic Art by the scholar-collector David Khalili, who had taken his doctorate at the School. This was filled by Michael Rogers, translated from the British Museum, whose formidable range of scholarship – he was already an FBA – was focused on the Ottoman period. The archaeology of the Islamic world was now covered by Geoffrey King, who was heavily engaged on surveys of the Arabian peninsula, while Anna Contadini worked on the decorative arts and manuscripts of Islam. When Rogers retired in 2000, his chair passed to Doris Behrens-Abouseif, whose specialism was the architecture of medieval Egypt. It is fitting that in the middle of this eventful period the department was able to move into fine and fitting new quarters in the Brunei Gallery.

If other regions were not so amply provided for, for Japan there was Tim Screech, a specialist in the arts of the Edo period (not excluding its pornography), for South Asia Giles Tillotson, whose research interests extended themselves from Mughal architecture to the interplay of British and Indian art and design, and for South East Asia Elizabeth Moore, who wrote extensively on the temple complexes of Cambodia, Burma and Thailand. Africa presented a very different subject matter, not so much because its art was intrinsically different, but because the canons for its analysis were much less formed, and the boundaries 'between 'art' and other manifestations of culture were less sharply defined. Ethnographic approaches were more necessary for the arts of Africa than for other regions, and the distinction between the work of 'traditional' and of contemporary artists was liable to break down. So it was that John Picton (who himself specialized in textiles, masquerade and contemporary art) played a major role in defining the subject in the international arena – for which in 2001 he received a rare lifetime Leadership Award from the African Arts Association in the USA. A second Africanist appointed in 1995, Tania Tribe, worked on the arts of Ethiopia and of the African diaspora, and shared with several others a thematic concern with the artistic import of colonialism and modernity.

The move to departmental status was accompanied by a significant shift in the character of the undergraduate degree. Up to the 1980s, when only a handful of students graduated in each year, the degree was predominantly archaeological, with 30 percent of its content – the more technical parts of the discipline – supplied externally from the Institute of Archaeology. With the fourfold rise of numbers that happened in the early 1990s, the degree needed to be completely reconstructed, and it became principally one in art history. While the distinctive appeal of the SOAS degree would still lie in the unequalled range of access it gave to the arts of Asia and Africa, it was also deemed crucial that there be a stronger common first-year grounding in the theoretical basis of the discipline: such topics as the psychology of perception, iconography, concepts of form and style, semiotics, and structuralism. So successful were these measures that in a Teaching Quality Audit in 1998 the department secured 24 points out of 24 for its courses. It was still possible for students to take a more conventional History of Art course, which SOAS and UCL shared 50:50, but the great majority of students went for SOAS's own Art and Archaeology degree, either singly or in combination.

A distinctive feature of Art and Archaeology is the routine involvement of its staff with the 'art world' beyond the academy in its various forms: with connoisseurs, museums, exhibitions and auction houses. Several members of the Department contributed to the series of events and exhibitions organized for 'Africa 95'. During the 1990s a full-fee Diploma course had been run in conjunction with Sotheby's, and though this was later taken over by the British Museum, many staff retained active links with it, as with other museums such as the Victoria and Albert. Several Circles of amateurs of the arts of particular regions – Islamic, Indian and Inner Asia – were formally associated with the Department, providing a means of outreach to the wider public. So, of course, did the Percival David collection and the facilities of the Brunei Gallery, though here the question was whether they might not be better integrated with the teaching and research functions of the Department. Throughout its first decade, Art and Archaeology rapidly gained a strong reputation for itself, with a Grade 5 in the RAEs of 1992 and 1996. Its fall to a Grade 3a in the 2001 RAE came as an unexpected shock and led to much heart-searching. The encouragement of a more collective research culture was felt to be part of the answer.

Study of Religions

It is probably true that some research and teaching on religion takes place in almost every department of the School (except perhaps Economics and Linguistics). The centrality of religious belief and ritual in the life of small-scale societies, even though they lacked the concept of 'religion'; the religious basis of Islamic and Hindu law; the ritual function of most ancient and tribal art and music; the role of priests as the custodians of writing systems and literature; the prominence of religious identity as a basis of social conflict throughout Asia and Africa: all these testify to the importance of the study of religion (or religions) at SOAS. Yet the School's authorities were long opposed to the establishment of posts expressly dedicated to the study of religion, on the grounds of its potentially divisive character. A partial exception was the Jordan Lectures on Comparative Religion, funded by a bequest, which had been given every few years since 1951. While most major religious scholarship came out of the regional departments – Mary Boyce's magisterial *History of Zoroastrianism* (Volume I, 1976) from the Near and Middle East Department, for example – it was historians who took the lead in realizing the potential of these unorganized riches.

When in the low years of the early 1980s the School looked to build up student numbers in areas of low demand, religious studies was seen as one way forward.

The introduction of course-unit BA degrees and the MA in Area Studies created niches for individual course options on particular religions, which were actively promoted by the then Senior Tutor, Humphrey Fisher. In 1982 the Yapp Report noted that no less than 40 teachers of the School had courses listed under the aegis of the Consultative Panel in Religion and Philosophy; and it envisaged a staff complement of 4.5 joint posts, with history or with languages. From 1984 a growing trickle of students began to graduate with joint degrees of which 'Religious Studies' was one half; but the first striking success came in 1986, when twelve students graduated with an MA in 'Oriental and African Religious Studies'. In 1985 the informal Panel had given way to a formal Centre of Religion and Philosophy, along the lines of those already existing for Music Studies and Art and Archaeology, under the chairmanship of the historian Richard Gray. By the early 1990s, with the precipitate rise in undergraduate numbers and with the blooming precedent of Art and Archaeology, the scale of the Centre's activities made it seem obvious to most people that it should go the further stage and become a fully fledged department, which it eventually did in 1992. The role of Humphrey Fisher in establishing Religious Studies at SOAS during the 1980s was absolutely crucial, though ironically as Chair of the Centre he had been opposed to departmental status for the study of religions and wished to retain for it a wide cross-disciplinary and interdepartmental role.

Because it was set up in the way and at the time that it was, the Department could not at once realize its objective: to provide coverage of all the major religious traditions of Asia and Africa around a 'core' of the theory-and-method relevant to the Study of Religions. It had a harder birth than Art and Archaeology since, though two new exclusive posts were created, the rest of its dozen or so staff continued to keep half a foothold in their prior departments. The task of building the core and pulling together the range of expertise in particular traditions (where SOAS was already quite unequalled) fell to the new Head, John Hinnells – already a prominent figure in the world of 'religious studies' – who set about it with vigour, generating some friction in the process. It was he who insisted on the name 'Study of Religions', rather than 'Religious Studies' or 'Comparative Religion' for the new department. The former was felt to be too vague and to imply the 'theology plus' character of most British departments in the field, while the latter, although a distinct and reputable activity, was not what most of the staff did, which was to work on a particular tradition. While hermeneutic and textual methods were already well encompassed, the provision of the ethnographic and social scientific ones crucial to the study of contemporary religion came later from the appointment, first of an LSE-trained sociologist and then of a SOAS-trained anthropologist.

Studies in the major religious traditions of Asia, while already strong in the School, were not evenly represented in the department. Most distinctive was a spectrum that ran from Iranian religion through the Parsis – Hinnells' specialism – into India, where Julia Leslie's studies of gender and Hinduism deserve particular mention. Sikhism and Jainism were not neglected. Then on again, via Piatigorsky's work on ancient Indian religion, to Buddhism, with most emphasis on its northern, Mahayana branch: Tadeusz Skorupski's research on the texts of Tibetan Buddhism, the historian Tim Barrett's studies of the multiple religions of mediaeval China, and various other lines of work on Japanese and Chinese religion, both medieval and modern. Japanese funds later permitted the endowment of a post in Theravada Buddhism. The robed monks and nuns often to be seen about the Department were a token, not just of its particular strength in Buddhist studies, but of a fundamental aim of its research and teaching generally: to encourage a creative interplay between the academic study of the great religions of Asia from the outside and their internal traditions of piety and scholarship. This openness has not only drawn research students but also facilitated fundraising from Asian religious communities, since their leaders are attracted by the idea of having a 'showcase' for the cultural riches of their traditions at SOAS. The bronze effigy of the ancient sage Tiruvalluvar, donated by the south Indian state of Tamilnadu, which graces the walkway though to Woburn Square, may be taken as an iconic reminder of this.

It is probable that Islam has engaged the interest of more staff across the School than any other religion, but it presented a unique problem to the Department of the Study of Religions. What at the time was the largest research grant ever awarded to the School, for the 'Islam in Modern Africa' project of 1987-92, funded by a British Academy/Leverhulme grant, was put together by staff in the Departments of Politics (Donal Cruise O'Brien), Anthropology (David Parkin) and Africa (Louis Brenner) as well as at University College – but no textual Islamicist. And it remained the case that the principal teachers of Islamic topics all have their primary anchorage outside Study of Religions in other departments, either in History or in the Near and Middle East Department. The intimate connection between Islamic and Koranic studies, and the absolute dependence of the latter on Classical Arabic, means that those who are involved in exegetical and critical work on Islamic texts remain strongly rooted in Near and Middle East. Consequently, Islam remains less fully integrated in Study of Religions than the other major traditions.

The position of Christianity and of the African religions has been different again. Compared with most other departments of religious studies, what makes SOAS's unique is that it is not linked to, or an extension from, Christian theology. On the other hand Christianity, misleadingly viewed as a 'European' religion, had been regarded as falling outside the School's remit, but now needed to be properly brought on board as a religion with many millions of adherents in Africa and Asia. So a post in Oriental Christianity was created for the new department, and held with much promise for a few years by Andrew Palmer, whose research embraced both the early Syriac church and the Suroyo diaspora of today. As for Africa, its roots went back to a seminar run by Gray back in 1972-73 on 'Christianity in Post-Colonial Africa' in connection with a Leverhulme fellowship on the topic held by Adrian Hastings. This was picked up twenty years later with a further Leverhulme project on Christianity and civil society in Africa, directed by Peel and Hastings (by then professor at Leeds), which brought Paul Gifford to SOAS. In 1997 he joined the staff as a lecturer in African Christianity. The indigenous religions of Africa were covered by Louis Brenner (otherwise a historian of West African Islam) from his base in the Africa Department.

The late 1990s brought a period of uncertainty and turbulence, with the sudden departure of a cluster of staff, but then stabilization and resumed growth – some ten appointments since 1999 – under the next two Heads of Department, Simon Weightman, an Indologist, and Brian Bocking, a specialist in East Asian religions appointed as the new professor. The attachment of the London School of Jewish Studies in 2000 added, for a while, to the research strength and the comparative range of the Department. The growth of research students was such that by the early 2000s Religions came to outstrip all other departments: 60 to70 in all, the majority of them working on Buddhism or Indian religions. And with its six MA courses – two generic (one of these being on religion and gender) and four on specific regions or traditions – the department established a unique reputation in its field, alike for the range of its coverage of religions beyond Europe and for the cultural depth in which they could be studied. In quality too, it proved itself by gaining a Grade 5 in both the 1996 and 2001 RAEs.

Music

There had long been a sprinkling of staff with an interest in music, particularly Indian music, usually linked with language teaching, though they were unevenly spread. In the early 1970s, when it still had no post in art, the Africa Department had a post dedicated to 'African musical studies'. Then there was David Rycroft, a lecturer in Bantu languages, who conducted research on Zulu music and actually composed the Swaziland national anthem. Owen Wright taught Arabic, but had his main research interest in the history of music in the Middle East. In 1979 Music Studies was constituted as a cross-departmental Centre, with Wright as its Chairman; and Richard Widdess – the first member of staff to have a formal academic qualification in music – was appointed to a post exclusively in classical Indian music. Throughout the 1980s, though barely a handful of students took even a joint degree in music, many took music units as part of other BA degrees, or as a subject in the MA (Area Studies) degrees; and the ethnomusicology course attracted students taking the BMus at King's College.

Of all the sub-disciplines of music, ethnomusicology was the School's particular forte. It was strengthened by the arrival in 1987 of David Hughes, a specialist in Japan who had a toehold in Anthropology, and an MMus in Ethnomusicology was instituted. Two more appointments in the early 1990s – of Lucy Durán, an experienced journalist and broadcaster on Caribbean and West African music, who had done many years research on Malian *kora* performance, and of Keith Howard in Korean Studies, whose interests combined music and shamanism – consolidated the trend. Soon it was felt that, with five staff, a critical mass had been reached and that the Music Centre could move towards departmental status. Plans for a BA in Music Studies – which attracted a high unit of Teaching Grant – came to fruition in 1996, and further impetus was given by its success in gaining a Grade 5* in the 1996 RAE. Departmental status finally came in 1998, with Howard as its first Head, shortly followed by Widdess. By the end of the 1990s, further appointments in Chinese and in Jewish music gave, at least temporarily, coverage to nearly all of SOAS's principal regions. A Grade 5 in the 2001 RAE was capped by its success, as the centre of a consortium with other universities, in gaining funding from the Arts and Humanities Research Board for a Centre for Cross-Cultural Music and Dance Performance.

A gamelan performance

Its rapid growth in a period of financial stringency left the Music Department seriously ill-equipped in terms of such essential facilities as an up-to-date recording studio and soundproofed practice rooms, but the award of the AHRB Centre award enabled much to be done to supply the gaps. Performance – whether in practice or as an object of theoretical understanding – is indeed the keynote of the aspirations of the Department. Music has a higher profile in the School than its size might imply. The music-making it encourages draws in other students than those taking music degrees. It is not just the sound of the gamelan or African drums echoing along the corridors at certain times, but the spirited performances – ranging from Jewish klezmer music to performances on the Chinese *pipa* (lute) and *guqin* (zither) – which have come to be an essential feature of the School's degree ceremonies. And no other department could combine a modest little earner for itself with such an attractive advertisement for the School's mission as the Music Department has done with its compact discs of Asian and African music entitled 'Oceans of the Heart'.

Conclusion

In the course of 2002 SOAS underwent a major re-organization. Departments were grouped into three Faculties, with the five treated here being allotted to a Faculty of Arts and Humanities, whose newly appointed Dean was Tom Tomlinson, an economic historian of South Asia. The main academic argument advanced for faculties was that they would encourage greater 'synergy' between departments. Whether or not that comes to pass, it can hardly be said that the one-tier pre-faculty structure prevented co-operation among staff across the whole range of the School. That was exactly how the Departments of Art and Archaeology, Study of Religions and Music all originated, as well as a major research initiative like the 'Islam in Modern Africa' project. Such collaborative projects depend essentially on the intellectual interests of active staff, though of course they may be facilitated or hindered by institutional structures. Indeed, since faculties necessarily erect barriers of a kind that had not existed before, there is the possibility that they may actually make synergy more difficult between departments now placed in different faculties.

The Department which was put in the most difficult situation by the introduction of faculties was undoubtedly Anthropology. Though it is conventionally (and by bodies like the ESRC and the British Academy) regarded as a 'social science', it opted for the Faculty of Arts and Humanities, partly because of the prevailing theoretical stance of most of its members' work, which was more hermeneutic than positivist. Yet it remained the case that others had stronger links with the social sciences through Development Studies or with languages and cultures through Media Studies. For the Faculty of Arts and Humanities, though it contains a group of departments which in recent years have been on average the School's most distinguished – at least in terms of RAE ratings – is something of a residual category, with a weaker overall rationale than the other Faculties. It does not have a distinctive intellectual agenda of its own like the role of 'the social sciences' in development, nor can it offer anything like the solution to shared problems which many staff in the fragmented language departments have long wanted.

But what gave academic staff most pause was the abolition of department offices. This arose less from the practical inconvenience of the siting of the Faculty office in some cases several floors away or even in another building, or from the diminished level of administrative support available to them, than from its social consequences. The unsung heroines in the history of many departments have been their long-serving secretaries. It was precisely their closeness to 'their' department that gave them a knowledge of its specific personalities, needs and problems that enabled them both to give an irreplaceable service to their academic colleagues, and to perform a pivotal role as a source of benign gossip and friendly informed advice to students. If SOAS is remembered by former students as a particularly intimate institution, this is owed in no small measure to the atmosphere in a good department office, a place of informal encounter for all its members, both staff and students. It was widely felt that with their disappearance something vital had been torn out of the corporate life of the School.

6

The social sciences: Structural change and its contradictions

Terence J. Byres

The social sciences at SOAS

The authoritative *Encyclopaedia of the Social Sciences* includes within its remit the following disciplines: anthropology, economics, geography, history, law, political science, psychiatry, psychology, sociology, and statistics. That is a wide, but justifiable, definition of the social sciences, to which one might now add development studies. SOAS has had all of these represented departmentally, with the exception of psychiatry, psychology, and statistics, although statistics is, of course, taught in the different social sciences, especially in economics. In the 1960s, the then Director, C.H. Philips, did suggest the desirability of creating a Department of Psychology, but that did not come to pass. For the purposes of this chapter, the 'social sciences' are taken more narrowly than the foregoing classification, and are deemed to cover development studies, economics, geography, political science, and law. Curiously, the outsider might think, they do not include anthropology and sociology, which, in SOAS terms, we take as a collective unit (although the two exist separately elsewhere) and which are covered in the previous chapter on the Arts and Humanities by J. D. Y. Peel. That they form part of the social sciences is too obvious to need elaboration. Nor do they include history, a more understandable omission, although history's kinship with the social sciences is clear.

The social sciences emerged formally at SOAS when the Governing Body, in 1961, instituted a Department of Economic and Political Studies with effect from 1 January 1962, and from the same date renamed the Department of Cultural Anthropology as the Department of Anthropology and Sociology. The Department of Economic and Political Studies took up residence in 24 Woburn Square on 1 May 1962. This was the bridgehead that allowed full entry for the social sciences. The way was clear and the barbarian troops landed. The planting of the 'sociology' flag was a clear declaration of intent – a staking out of territory: for a social sciences presence without sociology was incomplete. SOAS would never be the same again and its character was about to change, fundamentally and irrevocably.

Each of the disciplines noted above as having had an existence in SOAS exists currently as a separate department with the exception of Geography, which has recently migrated to King's College, London (departing, officially, on 1 August 2001). My concern is to consider the emergence and development of the social sciences in the School over the four decades between 1962 and 2002: to capture something of their powerful impact on the School's character and structure; to give a flavour of their nature and distinctiveness; to convey the contradictions they have embodied, the challenges they have faced, and their responses to those challenges. As a necessary preliminary we need to place them in historical context. But first we may note the peculiar demands upon social scientists at SOAS, who pursue a serious regional interest, conduct scholarly research on their chosen region, and contribute to both undergraduate and postgraduate teaching programmes. In a recent history of the SOAS Law Department, Ian Edge captures this position well, observing that 'Generally, members of the department will have attained their culture-specific orientation before arriving in the department but, in the past, time and effort was expended in developing such expertise within the department. As this generally meant learning a difficult non-Western language, there was often a considerable period of time before establishment as a recognized scholar.'

The same is true, by and large, for the other social sciences. These obligations and time lags were especially important in the early years of the social sciences (certainly in the 1960s and 1970s), when initial expertise was acquired largely by training fellows with no previous knowledge of Asia or Africa. That diminished with the passage of time, although such appointments were still being made even in the late 1980s, albeit rarely by then. By contrast, by the 1990s, it was more or less exclusively scholars established in the field who were appointed. We may further point to the tensions that may exist between regional commitment and the maintenance of disciplinary expertise (including a familiarity with theoretical developments) in fast-changing disciplines. Each is important, and the latter is necessary both for the quality of research on the region and for the disciplinary courses that need to be taught as an essential part of both undergraduate and postgraduate degree programmes.

The Hayter years, 1959-67

We were brothers all
In honour, or in one community
Scholars and gentlemen
William Wordsworth

Edith's problem is that she is not a gentleman
Bernard Lewis

As Head of History in the immediate post-war years, C. H. Philips had presided over a substantial increase in the size of his Department. As Director of SOAS from 1957 until 1976, he grasped, with great energy and vision, the opportunities that presented themselves under the Scarbrough Report. Against considerable internal opposition, he brought the social sciences into SOAS as a significant presence, so securing one of the greatest changes in the School's academic composition and orientation. He had a vision of what SOAS should be as a rounded academic institution, a liberal vision that included the social sciences and history as equal partners with the language and culture departments. As part of that vision, the social sciences were to attract significant numbers of undergraduate and postgraduate students and thereby secure the School's future. Within the social sciences, economics was assigned a leading, general role, while geography, because it was so widely taught in British schools, was thought to be of particular significance in attracting undergraduates to the School.

The Department of Economic and Political Studies represented the first major thrust in the Philips offensive. Its origins lie in 1959, when, with $1 million obtained from the Ford Foundation, three appointments to Research Fellowships in economic history were made at SOAS: Kenneth Walker (China); Malcolm Caldwell (South East Asia); and Seymour Broadbridge (Japan). All were under thirty years old at the time, and these, for Philips, were the shock troops of the new order. The view was: let them sit in the Department of History until the new department, or departments, were formed; and this was legitimized by making the appointments initially in economic history. But the real initiative lay in economics, which was to lead the new social science offensive at SOAS. In addition to these new appointees, there were already in the Department of History three political historians willing to give up their label as historians and pursue contemporary 'political studies' – Hugh Tinker (for South and South East Asia), Jack Gray (China) and S. R. Mehrotra (India).

By 1960 a Department of Economic and Political Studies had become an open *quaesitum*. The nucleus for a new department existed, except that Caldwell elected to remain in History. One might have expected two separate departments. Economics and Politics, after all, then existed, as they do now, as quite distinct disciplines in many British universities. An innocent outsider might have assumed that the intended department represented an imaginative effort to secure a creative synergy between the disciplines: an 'interdisciplinarity' in which a joint political economy of development would be pursued; but such an assumption would have been false. Instead, the combined department was a concession to the existing balance of power in SOAS. Determined to introduce formally both economics and politics, Philips calculated that while he might get away with one new social science department and one new Head, in a system controlled by Heads appointed without term, he would not escape with two. Two might have tilted the balance too far against the then dominant language department Heads and would have been fiercely opposed by them.

A senior and respected scholar was needed to lead the new department, and a powerful figure duly appeared in Edith Penrose, an economist of growing stature. In 1959, a book that would forge for her a formidable reputation, *The Theory of the Growth of the Firm*, was published. Indeed, the 'Penrosian firm' has now become part of the vocabulary of economics. The page proofs were read by one of the great figures in Cambridge economics, Joan Robinson, who was impressed. She asked Edith to come to Cambridge to be interviewed for an appointment there, and Edith duly did so. But Joan Robinson's husband, E. A. G. Robinson, was less impressed and no job was proffered. As Philips pursued his search for a department Head at SOAS, she was about to be appointed at LSE. In his quest for someone of sufficient authority, he turned 'for advice… to an old friend, Lord Robbins, the doyen of economic studies at the LSE… who had the bright idea of negotiating the appointment jointly at our two colleges of Dr Edith Penrose, an American then engaged in research into Middle Eastern oil economics at Johns Hopkins University in the United States'. She was appointed in 1960 to a joint readership with LSE, with special reference to the Near and Middle East, and duly installed as first Head of the new department.

Other appointments were soon made. Two of these, with a future Department of Geography in mind, were geographers of the Middle East: Keith McLachlan (as a research fellow) and J. H. G. Lebon (a senior fellow). In Economics, P. K. O'Brien (Middle East) and T. J. Byres (South Asia) had also been appointed. Such was the base that existed in 1962, when the new department was opened, secured by the money made available by the government in response to the recommendations of the Hayter Report of 1961. Morale was high. With a pioneering spirit abroad, there was a sense of exhilaration among the economists at grappling with a new, exciting and rapidly growing subject, the economics of development, among those in politics at confronting a barely developed politics of development; and among the Training Fellows in both subjects as they taught themselves the rudiments of their chosen regions and began to pursue research seriously.

Elsewhere in the School's growing social sciences, the Law Department in1962 had twelve members of staff and was headed by J. N. D. Anderson, 'the leading British scholar of Islamic law' (according to J. S. Read). It was, by then, a well-established, mature department: 'an unusual Law Department, founded by a group of unusual people' (in the words of Ian Edge), with a considerable reputation and much scholarly energy. Noel Coulson, appointed in 1954, 'made the department the leading international centre of scholarship in Islamic law', while A. Gledhill and J. D. M. Derrett made 'complementary contributions to the reputation of the department in the laws of India and Pakistan'. The department was especially dynamic in the field of African law that had been established by Antony Allott, and whose practitioners included James Read. Tony Allott had already started in 1957 the *Journal of African Law*, the first journal devoted exclusively to its subject. He edited it for many years and it continues to flourish. Other members included Henry McAleavy (China) and E. Cotran (Africa).

The years from 1962 to 1967 were the 'golden years' of Hayter expansion. The eight members of the Economic and Political Studies Department (five in Economics, three in Politics) rapidly grew to twenty (eleven in Economics and nine in Politics). In Edith Penrose, Economics had the 'senior economist ...with international standing' sought by Philips to 'lead' the assembled group of young economists (or would-be economists). A further batch of promising young scholars was appointed to Research Fellowships in Economics, including, between 1962 and 1967, Christopher Howe (China), Peter Ayre (South East Asia), Bill Warren (Africa, south of the Sahara), and Robert Mabro (Middle East). In addition, Biplab Dasgupta was appointed as a Temporary Lecturer in Statistics in 1966 (the first non-regional appointment to be made) and by 1967 had been made 'permanent'. Of these appointees, only Warren and Dasgupta had previously done academic work on developing economies.

Penrose also had the task of leading the political scientists, but she had no expertise in that area. Senior expertise in political science was clearly necessary and the Department already had, in Hugh Tinker, a senior figure. He was the first Professor of Politics from 1963, but had no training in political science. Here was apparent, then, the clear weakness of gathering together a group of historians with an interest in political history but no training in political science. In 1962 there was no trained political scientist within the Department and the School had to acquire a senior political scientist from elsewhere. The choice fell on P. J. Vatikiotis, then Professor of Government at the University of Indiana, and a specialist on the Middle East, who was appointed in 1963. A third Professor of Politics was appointed in 1967. This was Stuart Schram, an established scholar on China, who would become the acknowledged Western authority on the life and political thought of Mao Tse-tung. Schram was the first Director of the Contemporary China Institute, and at that time the School also acquired the *China Quarterly*, whose first editor was David Wilson (the future governor of Hong Kong). Between 1963 and 1967 six new, young scholars were appointed in Politics, including Dennis Dalton (India), Donal Cruise O'Brien (Africa), and Abbas Kelidar (Middle East). The appointment of Dennis Dalton was especially important for the creation of a political studies programme. He brought to SOAS a serious concern with political theory, contributing to a course on Political Theory and teaching a Political Ideology course that brought distinction, coherence and intellectual quality to the Politics MSc.

Edith Penrose remained as Head of Department throughout the 1960s, finally resigning that post in June 1969. She pursued, from the outset, democratic practices. There were frequent department meetings, at which issues were discussed that in other SOAS departments were strictly the preserve of the Head. She delegated tasks to young academics that other Heads dealt with themselves, and she carried to the Heads of Departments Committee, then the fount of all power, decisions argued out in the department, in a way then unique in SOAS. But life was not necessarily placid for members of the department, young or old, economists or political scientists. With her direct and confrontational style, both privately and in seminars, and believing that the way to get the best out of people was to challenge them constantly and create for them the maximum insecurity, she was the living embodiment of a kind of Schumpeterian creative destruction. Her seminar style was aggressive; her instinct was always to go for the jugular, quite ruthlessly, whomsoever, high or low, she was confronting. But it was a wholly democratic aggression: the other Heads experienced it as much as anyone else, and must have been bewildered at quite how to handle her. Even the Director was not exempt. Lord Robbins, that most austere and icily calm of academic Brahmins, once said to her: 'Edith, why is it that within ten minutes of starting a conversation with you, I find myself invariably raising my voice?'

The intellectual energy of the Department, in those 'golden' years had already begun to show. In an important SOAS initiative, T. J. Byres had suggested to Frank Cass that a new development journal should be instituted, the only one then active being *Economic Development and Cultural Change*. Cass agreed and the first editor of the new *Journal of Development Studies* was Edith Penrose. The first issue appeared in 1964, and there was strong involvement from both the economics and politics sides of the Department until 1973, with Howe and Cruise O'Brien taking stints as the managing editor and Dalton and Byres involved editorially. From these modest beginnings at SOAS, it has grown to become one of the leading development journals.

New appointments were made in Law, but they grew by only one in net terms (from twelve to thirteen). Among its distinguished members, J. D. M. Derrett stands out as one who put an indelible stamp upon SOAS at the time. He was a SOAS eccentric from a bygone age. Werner Menski cites the reputation of Derrett among Indian scholars as 'that *rishi* sitting on the bank of the Thames' and describes his 'love-hate relationship with India'. His legal writing was prolific and he wore that erudition along with an equally abundant biblical scholarship, as the list of staff publications in the Annual Report of the Governing Body impressively revealed year after year. He managed to combine the two areas of his scholarship in a remarkable, and beautifully delivered, inaugural lecture given in 1966, entitled 'An Oriental Lawyer Looks at the Trial of Jesus Christ and the Doctrine of Redemption'. One attended meetings at which he would be present – whether of the Academic Board, or South Asia seminars, or School committees – with expectation, since his utterances could be vitriolic, insightful or outrageous, but never dull. He was an unforgettable figure.

The Department of Geography was established in 1965, with C. A. Fisher as its first Head. The two geographers of 1962 had grown to eight by 1967. They included J. A. (Tony) Allan, a Research Officer who would prove to be a long-standing and distinguished member of the School, and John Sargent, a Japan specialist. Yet, the kind of energy generated in Economics, Politics and Law was somehow not in evidence in Geography. Life was more tranquil than in Economics and Politics, but along with the tranquillity came a lack of intellectual leadership. With hindsight, looking back over the past four decades, one might observe that of all the social science departments at SOAS, Geography was the one that proved most deficient in that kind of leadership.

There was at that time no undergraduate teaching in the Department of Economic and Political Studies because of the absence of a suitable accommodation and facilities (including a library). But MSc programmes were quickly established in both disciplines, beginning with a few entrants in 1963 and increasing numbers thereafter, and an active part was played in the new Area Studies programmes launched in 1966. The MSc programmes proved successful and, as they grew, attracted high-quality students; and it was in those early Area Studies programmes that the new social scientists first taught comprehensive courses on their regions. Yet, from the outset there was limited communication between the two disciplines. Initially, there was a joint seminar, attended by all members of the department, but it did not last very long. Interdisciplinarity did not flourish. Likewise, Geography did no undergraduate teaching, but in 1967 established a new MSc in the Geography of Monsoon Asia and contributed actively to Area Studies MA teaching. Law participated only marginally in the Hayter expansion. The department gave instruction for the LLM, but as yet had no undergraduate degree.

Between 1962 and 1967, staff numbers at the School rose from 178 to 227. Total staff in the social sciences (including Anthropology and Sociology) grew from 30 to 53, an increase of 77 percent. History also shared in that expansion, rising from 23 to 32, or by 39 percent. Thus, the social sciences plus History rose substantially from 53 to 85, with the non-social science staff growing, too, from 125 to 142. Structural change was proceeding rapidly, with the proportion of social science staff rising from 17 to 23 per cent of total staff, and social science plus History from 30 to 37 percent. Philips had thereby secured one of his main objectives; but by the late 1960s the 'golden years' of Hayter expansion were already coming to an end.

Hard times and soldiering through, 1967-88

The old is dying and the new cannot be born
Antonio Gramsci

Between 1967 and 1987 there was a steady downward trend in total School staff: from 227 to 165. Within that decline, while language and culture staff fell from 142 to 82 (by 42 percent), social science numbers (without History) actually rose, from 53 to 59 (by 11 percent). Within the individual departments change was uneven. Economics fared badly, declining from its post-1962 peak of eleven to just nine in 1987; while Politics added one member of staff, rising from nine in 1967 to ten in 1987. Law grew from thirteen to fifteen; Geography from eight to twelve; and Anthropology and Sociology from twelve to thirteen. History, after rising to a high point of 35 in the mid-1970s, fell back to 24 in 1987. What is clear in all this detail is a continuing process of structural change, with the social sciences rising from 23 percent to 36 percent of the School's academic staff, and, if we add History to 50 percent. Here was a true watershed. The double Philips transformation, involving first History and then the social sciences, had been secured. The social sciences were now well and truly woven into the fabric of the School and SOAS was no longer an institution pursuing largely the study of language and literature. It had cast off its 'Orientalist' image.

However, one unfortunate event cast a long shadow throughout this whole period. This was the 'Dasgupta Affair', which erupted in the Department of Economic and Political Studies and had reverberations across the School. The story of the 'Dasgupta Affair' is long, complex and controversial. Dasgupta, who was on a probationary contract, was told, on returning from study-leave in October 1971 and without any previous warning, that his contract would not be renewed. In effect, he was sacked. The way in which this was done, the absence of concrete grounds for non-renewal, the lack of any regard for due process, and the peremptory manner in which he was treated, caused outrage among some of Dasgupta's colleagues on both sides of the Department, grave disquiet throughout the School and nationally. Despite much protest, the original decision was upheld by the Governing Body at the end of June 1972 and Dasgupta left to take up a post at the Institute of Development Studies, Sussex. This is not the place to consider the details of the 'Affair', but it does merit recording, because of its repercussions in the Department of Economic and Political Studies. What had been a happy, co-operative department, albeit one in which there was no particular synergy between the two sections, became one that was badly divided. There was bitterness, ill-feeling and, in some instances, a breakdown in communication. Recovery would take a long time.

Philips remained as Director until 1976. He was succeeded by another historian, C. D. Cowan, who held office until 1989. As Richard Rathbone's chapter points out, it was Cowan's unfortunate fate to preside over an era of financial stringency and contraction that lasted for almost the whole of his directorship. The era of Heads of Department with apparent power and prolonged tenure remained, but whatever power they had was not, for the most part, deployed creatively. In Economic and Political Studies, Edith Penrose was succeeded by Ken Walker, who was Head from 1969 to 1985, followed briefly by Christopher Howe from 1986 to 1988. The 'Dasgupta Affair' continued to exert its influence until the end of this period. It had blighted activity in the Department. In Geography, Charles Fisher held on to the headship until 1981. In the second half of the 1970s, he was seriously ill and others – John Sargent and Dick Hodder – had to deputize for him. It would have been better for Geography had he handed over the headship earlier: initiatives were not taken and there was little sense of direction. He died in 1982. Dick Hodder succeeded him, only to take premature retirement in 1983. Geography thus lost its two professors and lacked purposive leadership. No further appointment to a professorship was made until Graham Chapman came to the School in 1988. In Law Norman Anderson remained as Head until 1971, when he handed over to Tony Allott. Anderson had been Head for eighteen years – which, according to Allott, were 'eighteen years of inspired leadership'. He bequeathed a department in good heart. Allott was Head until 1978, and, thereafter, apparently successfully, in succession, by Margaret Rogers, Noel Coulson and finally, in 1986, Jim Read. Of all the social science departments, Law showed the greatest dynamism.

There were some happy developments. As a result of initiatives in Economic and Political Studies and History, in January 1972 there was instituted the 'Peasants' seminar of the University of London. The initiatives were taken by T. J. Byres and Charles Curwen. The seminar ran until February 1989 and hosted 208 papers, and, in its heyday, it came to represent the leading academic forum in the United Kingdom for the discussion of agrarian political economy. It was attended by economists, political scientists, geographers, sociologists, historians and others. It was a genuinely interdisciplinary forum, succeeding, in this respect, where the Department of Economic and Political Studies had not. Outstanding established scholars in agrarian studies read papers, along with a large number of young scholars, at the start of their careers, many of whom are now luminaries in their fields. Out of it grew the *Journal of Peasant Studies*, edited by Byres, Curwen, and, to start off with, Teodor Shanin: the first issue appeared in October 1973. This, in its turn, became the leading international journal of agrarian political economy. The present Director of the School, Colin Bundy, addressed the seminar three times and was, for a time, a regular attender. It was addressed, too, by David Arnold, until recently the School's Pro-Director for Research, who took a keen interest in its proceedings.

Journal of Peasant Studies cover design

Morale throughout the School rose markedly when the new building and accompanying Library, long in the making and truly liberating in their coming, were occupied in May-June 1973. This made possible the introduction of full undergraduate teaching in the social sciences, brought a massive improvement in working conditions, and thereby greatly raised staff spirits. Indeed, the buildings' completion and occupation seemed to coincide with a dramatic revival of the School's financial fortunes. The years 1967-72 were 'an enforced period of consolidation' (according to the School's *Annual Report* for 1972-73), as the financial going got tough. In 1973, which took on the air of an *annus mirabilis*, things seemed to get far better. But, even as the sun shone on SOAS, dark clouds were gathering on the horizon. In 1973 Philips could articulate a heady vision, full of confidence and optimism for the future, including, for the social sciences, the possibility of an ambitious programme of demographic studies. By 1974, however, the mood had darkened once more. The buoyancy and hope of 1973 had gone and the School entered a period of financial crisis that would not ease until the late 1980s. There would be no programme of demographic studies.

In the late 1970s, Jeremy Cowan announced the need to reduce staff numbers. He discounted the possibility, discussed in the press, that the School might have to close altogether. There were two broad possible solutions: compulsory redundancies, that might have involved closing whole departments, or voluntary retirements. Indeed, there was informal discussion, around that time, as to whether some social science departments, among them Economic and Political Studies, might be closed. Whatever expedient was resorted to, Cowan stressed, the School that entered the 1990s was likely to be 'a leaner body than that which now exists'. In the event, the Government announced that it would finance a scheme for voluntary retirements, for senior university staff, and this was adopted in SOAS. The early retirement of senior staff began in 1982. In the five sessions, 1981-82 to 1985-86, there were 34 premature retirements. They included many outstanding scholars. It was a sad period. The cuts were, indeed, largely concentrated in the language departments. Of the 123 members of the language departments that were there in 1977, 23 (19 percent) departed. Six went from History, out of the 35 there in 1977 (17 percent). So the language departments and History suffered more or less equally in proportionate terms. Because of their relatively young age structure, the social sciences escaped quite lightly, with only five early departures (including Anthropology and Sociology), or 8 per cent of the 1977 total. Here was structural change by the blunt instrument of premature retirement.

None the less, in this period of retrenchment, there were several new arrivals who would make their careers in the School. Among others, in Economics, Robert Ash (China), Nigel Crook (India), and Caroline Dinwiddy (Statistics and Econometrics) were appointed; in Politics the appointments included David Taylor (South Asia), Richard Jeffries (West Africa), Tom Young (Africa), R. H. Taylor (South East Asia) and Charles Tripp (Middle East); the Geography Department added R. W. Bradnock (South Asia), B. W. Hodder (Africa), Philip Stott (South East Asia), Kathleen Baker (Africa), Deborah Potts (Africa), R. J. Wiltshire (Japan) and R. L. Edmonds (China). The Department of Law, happier in spirit than Economic and Political Studies, and without the premonitory rumblings that might be detected in Geography, grew somewhat. Among their appointments were Doreen Hinchcliffe (Islamic Law), Margaret Rogers (Africa), A. R. Dicks (China), Peter Slinn (Africa), S. F. R. Coldham (Africa), Ian Edge (Islamic and Middle East Law), W. F. Menski (South Asia) A. D. Huxley (South East Asia); followed in 1985 by D. C. Clark (Far East), Andrew Harding (South East Asia) and M. J. E. Palmer (East Asia).

It was in 1975 that the full panoply of social science undergraduate degrees was introduced, often in combination with other subjects. That, most certainly, ushered in a new era for the social sciences. The days of exclusively postgraduate departments had gone. In 1975 Law and Geography were the only social science departments in which there were, as yet, single subject degrees. By 1987 only Economics lacked such a degree. One can see a connection between the establishment of an undergraduate programme and the injection of some new dynamism. This can be seen clearly in one case, at least. In Law the realization of the Philips vision of social science undergraduate programmes proved to be invigorating and enhancing. The introduction of an undergraduate Law degree involved negotiation with bodies outside the School and, necessarily, some concessions, but to good purpose. Much negotiating with the legal professional bodies obtained the significant concession that even in the core subject of English law, up to 25 percent of the curriculum could be taught from non-English materials. Hence, contract law can use precedent from, say, East Africa; commercial law can look at developments in the Middle East and China; property and criminal law can use Commonwealth precedent and family law has considerable input from Africa, the Middle East and China. The undergraduate programme went from strength to strength as students realized that here was a different Law school presenting a different degree, although one which was recognized by the professional bodies for practical purposes. Here, then, in the Law case, is a true SOAS success story, grounded in a distinguished past and secured in a contemporary context.

Masters programmes had been established successfully by 1967 in all the social sciences. Such programmes are an extremely important part of a social science department's intellectual vitality, its outside reputation, and its legacy. Before the coming of the undergraduate programmes, these MScs were crucial. They were a central part of any dynamism that a department might have, and they continued to be so after 1967. There was no more successful MSc than that in Economics. That MSc was vigorous and flourishing through to the early 1970s; and the same was true of the MSc in Politics. Both MScs attracted excellent students and trained a number of outstanding development specialists. But in the 1970s the MScs in both Economics and Politics lost momentum and vitality. The Yapp Report (discussed elsewhere in this volume) noted in 1982 that in Economics, between 1973-74 and 1981-82, the intake fell from seventeen to seven, and that a similar situation existed in Politics. In Economics an attempt was made to address this by introducing in 1984-85 a joint MSc with University College in the Economics of Public Policy in Developed and Developing Countries. It did not prove successful, however, and the joint venture lasted for only three sessions. In 1987-88, for the first time since 1963, there was no MSc programme in Economics and for a further three sessions there would be no such MSc offered at SOAS.

Geography escaped criticism in the Yapp Report, but already it was experiencing problems with respect to its undergraduate recruitment and takers for its Masters programme. With the death of Charles Fisher in 1982 and the premature retirement of Dick Hodder in1983, it lost its two professors and, with them, rather lost its way. A new professor, Graham Chapman, was appointed in 1988, while Tony Allan became a professor in the same year. The former served as Head of Department from 1991 until 1994, when he resigned from the School; the latter never served as Head. There was one recommendation of the Yapp Report that was not acted upon at the time, but was a significant pointer to the future: that a Development Studies Masters degree should be initiated. It was suggested that a 'central core' should be established that 'could hold such a programme together' through the establishment of one or two full-time posts. Law, Anthropology and Economics were singled out as likely strong contributors to any future Development Studies programme. In fact, Development Studies did not come to pass until our next period but the seed was planted by the Yapp Report, and the initial shape of the Development Studies programme, when it did come about, was very much in the mould suggested there.

Success and failure in the social sciences, 1988-2002

No longer does an Orientalist try first to master the esoteric languages of the Orient; he begins instead as a trained social scientist and 'applies' his science to the Orient
Edward Said

1988 marks the start of a new era. C. D. Cowan was succeeded in 1989 by Michael McWilliam, who was Director until 1996. For the social sciences, his arrival was particularly important. With him came a period of far greater buoyancy, and, at last, a resumption of expansion. The whole School benefited from his leadership, but he was especially keen to see the social sciences grow. Trained as an economist and a former merchant banker, he was surprised at the small presence economics had in the School and resolved to see this change. He was similarly committed to the growth of the other social sciences.

The reading room of the Library

The Library at Finsbury Circus in the 1930s

The new entrance to the Library, 2003

The Byte2e@t café at Vernon Square

On the steps of the Brunei Gallery

An exhibition of African art at the Brunei Gallery

The Japanese garden at the Brunei Gallery

The cup-winning SOAS women's football team, 1998

A music class at SOAS with David Hughes

SOAS students at work

The Tamil sage Tiruvalluvar

In this last period, the School total academic staff rose from 165 in 1987 to 247 in 2002. That increase of 82 represented a rise of 50 percent. The dark days were over, although the challenges and pressures of the new era remained great. In the new financial environment, performance in the Research Assessment Exercise (RAE) became decisive for the funding and the reputation of individual departments, while pursuit of research or other grants, with their accompanying overheads, became integral to survival and growth. The Thatcherite agenda had been carried through with great success. Social science staff and History together rose from 83 to 118, and social sciences alone from 59 to 95 (by 42 percent and 61 percent respectively). In 1987, the proportion of social science and History staff had reached 50 percent, and that of the social sciences alone 36 percent. The former rose to 53 percent in 1992 and the latter to 41 percent. The change in the School's structure since 1962 had been dramatic. The overall rise of the social sciences (despite the departure of Geography in 2001) continued the structural transformation of the School initiated by Philips in the early 1960s. Forty years on, his legacy in this, as in so much else, is abundantly clear.

Behind these figures lay much change. The School itself has become qualitatively different and the social sciences themselves are, in several respects, transformed. In each of the social sciences, there is less emphasis on regional representation and balance, as disciplinary demands have received greater recognition – a clear outcome of both RAE considerations and the demands of teaching programmes. To a far greater extent than previously, the 'discipline' and the need to be recognized in disciplinary terms have dictated choices. Mastery of a 'difficult non-Western language' is no longer a binding commitment. A clear image of professional expertise has been sought, yet without abandoning the distinctiveness of the SOAS departments. That distinctiveness continues to be rooted in unrivalled scholarship on the countries of Asia and Africa, albeit not necessarily language-based. There were two new, bustling and financially rewarding activities among the social sciences: long-distance education and Development Studies, which emerged, eventually, as departments, while Geography, a department established in the 1960s, left SOAS altogether in this period.

A critical change came in Economic and Political Studies. Christopher Howe resigned as Head and was succeeded by R. H. Taylor in October 1988, the first political scientist to head the Department since its establishment in 1962. Byres became head of the Economics section. It soon became apparent that there was a majority within the Department in favour of dividing, with each section wishing to consolidate and pursue its disciplinary identity. The case was argued and accepted by the School, and the division became effective as of October 1990. After more than a quarter of a century, what had, in effect, been a barren union came to an end. Whatever possibilities existed for interdisciplinary activity had not been taken: that, no doubt, was an opportunity lost.

In 1988-89 and 1989-90 Economics began to put its house in order, a process that continued after the establishment of the new Department in 1990. By 1992 the Department had grown from the nine staff members of 1987 to fourteen; by 1997 it was sixteen, and eighteen by 2002. Economics at SOAS became larger and stronger than it had ever been before. Ken Walker, one of the earliest SOAS social science appointees, died in 1989, having made an outstanding contribution to scholarship on the Chinese rural economy. There followed a double blow when Caroline Dinwiddy, after whom one of the student residences is now named, died in an accident in late 1994, followed by Nigel Crook in 1995. They had both been committed and outstanding teachers, serious scholars, and part of the very backbone of the Department of Economics. The new appointments included Graham Dyer (Middle East), Anne Booth (South East Asia), Massoud Karshenas (Middle East), Costas Lapavitsas (Japan), John Sender (Africa), Ben Fine (South Africa), Mushtaq Khan (South Asia), Machiko Nissanke (Africa), Dic Lo (China), Jonathan Pincus (South East Asia), and Rathin Roy (South Asia). From being a small band of economists, the department became the largest concentration of development economists in any British university. Moreover, its true distinctiveness lies in the political economy practised by most of its members.

With the establishment of the new department an MSc programme was resumed. This proved very successful: MSc numbers rose from eleven in 1990-91 to 46 in 1993-94, and they have continued to rise. A new, dynamic family of MScs in Economics was created. In addition, a single-subject degree in Economics was introduced in 1992. Its introduction raised the Department's student intake, improved the quality of that intake, and, with the rising MSc numbers, gave the Department an altogether more respectable staff-student ratio. Total undergraduate numbers rose from 41 in 1989-90 to 112 in 1993-94. In November 1999 the Department, on the basis of a broad range of criteria, was placed top in a national ranking of economics departments published in *The Guardian*.

In the summer of 1990 Laurence Harris joined the department, and brought with him an exciting distance learning programme, which was a new venture for the

School: this involved an MSc in Financial Economics and was embodied in the Centre for International Education in Economics (CIEE). It had two members of staff initially, which, by 1997, had expanded to five. It grew into the Centre for Finance and Management Studies (CeFiMS), established in 2000, which two years later became the Department of Financial and Management Studies. It now awards internal degrees, currently has a staff of eight, and is quite separate from the Department of Economics. Two staff members who were employed to work for CIEE moved permanently to the Department of Economics: Hassan Hakimian (Middle East) and Sonali Deraniyagala (South Asia), while, in the reverse direction, Christopher Howe joined CeFiMS from Economics.

In 1991 a Centre for Development Studies was established and the School advertised for a Director of Development Studies. No particular disciplinary preference was stated. In the event, it was an economist, John Weeks (whose major regional concern was with Latin America) who was appointed. A BA in Development Studies was instituted in 1991; at the same time, an MA in Development Studies was inaugurated with John Weeks as its Director. The latter burgeoned, and in 1992 Deniz Kandiyoti, a sociologist with a research interest in the Middle East and Central Asia, was appointed. She bore a heavy load in the running of the postgraduate programme. The Department of Development Studies was established as a postgraduate-only department in 1996, with Lisa Croll (an anthropologist who works on China) as its first Head. In 2001 it had nine members of staff, which by 2002 had risen to twelve. A new, important social science presence had arrived, with staff in the whole range of social science disciplines. Its current Head, Henry Bernstein (East Africa and South Africa), had been appointed to the School in 1996 as a Professor of Development Studies, initially as part of another long-distance education programme. The other members of staff are presently: Christopher Cramer (Africa), Jonathan Goodhand (South and Central Asia), Tania Kaiser (East and West Africa and Sri Lanka), Ray Kiely (the Caribbean), Jens Lerche (South Asia), Carlos Oya (West and Southern Africa), Elaha Povey (Middle East), Alfredo Saad-Filho (Southern Africa and Latin America), and Subir Sinha (South Asia). In addition to taking over responsibility for undergraduate teaching from the departed Geographers, the Department now has a thriving Masters programme, by far the largest in the School, and the largest Development Studies Masters programme in the country. It is a vigorous centre of research in political economy and especially agrarian political economy. The editors of the successful *Journal of Peasant Studies*, Henry Bernstein and T. J. Byres (now retired and a Professorial Research Associate of the department), left its publisher, Frank Cass, in 2000, and in 2001 started, this time with Blackwell, a new journal, the *Journal of Agrarian Change*.

In Law staff numbers had risen to eighteen by 1992. They rose appreciably more in 1993-94, with the arrival of FIELD – the Foundation for International Environmental Law and Development – which remained at SOAS until 2001. Even with its departure the steadily expanding department had raised its staff to 22 by 2002. Among the appointments have been Martin Lau (South Asia), Nicholas Foster (Commercial Law), Catherine Jenkins (South Africa), Fareda Banda (Family Law), Matthew Craven (Public International Law), Lynn Welchman (Islamic and Middle Eastern Law), Scott Newton (Central Asia), Sanzu Zhu (China), and Makeen F. Makeen (Commercial Law). It can, with truth, be said some fifty years after its founding, that 'the SOAS Law Department is in many ways a unique law department' (to quote Ian Edge) and has made, and (in the words of Jim Read) continues to make, 'a distinctive contribution to the texture of British legal education'. It continues to be, too, as in the past, distinguished, vibrant and full of character. It has played a major role in the development of new approaches in the field of comparative law. In 2000-01 it was recognized in *The Guardian* as providing the best undergraduate law programme in the United Kingdom and in the 2001 Research Assessment Exercise was rewarded with a 5 grade, the only SOAS social science department to achieve that prestigious ranking.

In Politics the 1987 staff of ten had risen to eighteen in 2002. As with Economics, going its separate way proved liberating. Like Economics, Politics established a new family of MScs that would prove highly successful and strengthened its undergraduate programme. In 1989 both P. J. Vatikiotis and Stuart Schram retired, and thus were the last links with the 1960s all but severed (Donal Cruise O'Brien is the last remaining from that era in Politics). Political Studies acquired an accomplished theorist in Sudipta Kaviraj, who joined the School from Jawaharlal Nehru University in Delhi in 1991; and in Kathryn Dean has a specialist in social theory and political ideologies, who was appointed in 1990. Some appointments in both Economics and Law had been made since the 1960s without regional reference. Kathryn Dean was the first in Politics of this kind, thus acknowledging the disciplinary needs of the department. Moreover, it now has that expertise in international politics recommended years earlier by the Yapp Report: with Stephen Hopgood and Mark Laffey as lecturers in that subject (again without specific regional reference). These and other members of the Politics Department, with support from other departments, have been particular influential in establishing a new and now thriving Centre for International Studies and Diplomacy, with Peter Slinn, formerly of the Law department as Director of its MA programme. Other appointments to Politics in this period have been: E. Kienle (Near and Middle East); William Hale (Turkey), Philip Deans (China), Timothy Springer (Japan), Tat Yang Kong (Korea), John T. Sidel (South East Asia), Lesley Connors (Japan), Stephen Heder (South East Asia), and Bhavna Dave (Central Asia). Like Law and Economics, Politics has begun to receive its accolades. In 1999 the SOAS Department was rated first equal among all Politics departments in the country by *The Guardian.*

Geography, by contrast, had experienced difficulty in recruiting both undergraduates and postgraduates from the late 1980s onwards, and uniquely among the social sciences at SOAS, its staff numbers remained stagnant after 1987. Most critically, it was suggested by HEFCE that it was too small to run an effectively rounded undergraduate degree. As indicated earlier, Geography appeared to lack the dynamism of the other SOAS social science departments. In an increasingly competitive academic environment, the Department seemed unable, without new appointments and a larger student and research base, to generate the requisite initiatives from within. It took over the administration of the Development Studies undergraduate degree and made some teaching input to it; but that alone could not make it a viable entity. It did introduce new MScs, which ironically by 2000 were showing some vitality. But it was too little, too late. In the end, both Royal Holloway and King's College were keen to absorb the SOAS department. It was King's that made the most attractive offer, and when it was put to the vote in the Department, a narrow majority voted in favour of going to King's.

In the annual SOAS *Our Year in Review* for 2000-01 the issue of Geography's departure was posed in terms of the need for restructuring within the discipline of Geography. 'The Geography Department', it noted, 'has engaged with the challenge of restructuring within the discipline by merging (as of 1 August 2001) with the Department of Geography of King's College, London.' As a result of the merger, the combined Department at King's now had over 30 research-active staff, 60 doctoral, 90 Masters and over 300 undergraduate students, thus representing 'the largest concentration in the United Kingdom of academic expertise on development geography and the environmental problems of Asia and Africa'. 'The merger agreement', it was further observed, 'protects and enhances the full range of masters and undergraduate degrees formerly taught at SOAS, including optional courses now available to students at both institutions.'

Perhaps the discipline of Geography did need restructuring. But, paradoxically, the original Philips vision was that *SOAS* (and not some other London college) should have the 'largest concentration in the United Kingdom of academic expertise on development geography and the environmental problems of Asia and Africa'. SOAS remains, in many respects, the most logical base for such a concentration, as it is by far the largest concentration of academic expertise in the UK on the history, economies, politics, law, and development problems in general of Asia and Africa. In this particular respect, at least, the social sciences at SOAS have proved to be sorely lacking. The SOAS geographers themselves had failed to take early initiatives on, for example, environmental problems, while the School, for its part, was not willing at a critical stage to take financial risks in making appointments that might have turned things round.

Conclusion

Brevis esse laboro,
Obscurus fio

It is when I am struggling to be brief
that I become unintelligible
Horace

I have had to represent a long and complex story in very short compass, omitting much that is important and fascinating, and oversimplifying, sometimes to the point (almost) of caricature. The development of the social sciences at SOAS has, inevitably, had its contradictions and disappointments, not all of which I have had space to record. The one major disciplinary casualty has been Geography. It is undeniable, however, that, on the whole, the emergence and development of the social sciences in SOAS, over the last forty years and more, has been a story of considerable success. They have proved, with the exception of Geography, to be a dynamic element in the School's fortunes, emerging, after the crisis years of 1967-88, as strong and buoyant. They have had considerable scholarly distinction, which I have not had space to discuss, and have grown to be a potent force. I am sure that they will go on to yet greater strength.

7

The SOAS Library and archives

Keith Webster and Rosemary Seton

The heart of the School

That SOAS should have a Library of international importance at its heart had been envisaged almost from the time at which the establishment of the School itself was first considered. During its first 50 years remarkable progress was made in creating a world-class research facility, in part through the Library's establishment from collections drawn from other Colleges of the University and elsewhere and in part through donations of significant collections and through greatly appreciated financial awards from the School's funders. Since the early history of the Library has been well documented in the account by A. Lodge of 'The History of the Library of the School of Oriental and African Studies' published in *University and Research Library Studies*, edited by W.L. Saunders (1968), this chapter outlines some of the main features of the Library's development over the past 35 years before concluding with a separate description of the archives.

In 1961 the Hayter Report, which considered the future of Asian, African and Slavonic studies, recommended that SOAS Library should be regarded as a national library, and given additional direct funding to support levels of staffing and collections far beyond those affordable to the School. By the end of the century the Library had expanded greatly, particularly after its move into the new building in 1973, and it now attracts thousands of scholars from around the world each year. The Parker Report rightly hailed the Library as 'the jewel in the School's crown'. Anyone who has been connected with SOAS will have strong memories of time spent in the Library – recollections of insights into new areas, or fears of impending examinations. But its place in the School has often gone beyond that of an academic service; it has served as a meeting place and was indeed reported in a 1990s survey by the Students' Union as the best place for students to find their dream date!

The growth of the Library

When the School was established in 1916 a Library was created through the transfer of relevant books and journals from the libraries of the London Institution and other libraries of the University of London. Early records indicate that the Library initially comprised some 9,000 volumes, and by the time the School moved to its new home in Bloomsbury this had grown to over 90,000 items. During the first 25 years of the School's existence the post of Librarian was held by the Director and it was not until 1940 that these two offices were separated. It was only in 1947 that the School appointed its first full-time Librarian, N. C. Sainsbury. He was succeeded in 1950 by J. D. Pearson who was to oversee a period of tremendous expansion during more than twenty years in post.

The original Library at the Bloomsbury site had been designed to accommodate some 100,000 volumes but the pace of collection development was such that its capacity had been exceeded by 1948. From 1949 the need for a new Library was a frequent refrain in annual reports and the combined effects of growth of academic activity in the School and improved supply of publications, particularly from China, presented further intense space pressures on the Library. The Library's collections were soon dispersed across varying locations both in the School, elsewhere in central London and at the University's Library Depository at Egham. Pressure had been growing for many years for the creation of a dedicated Library building, space for which had been identified immediately to the north of the main building.

Much work was carried out in the following twenty years to secure the necessary funds and in navigating many seemingly insurmountable central and local government barriers. Finally, in 1966, the University Grants Committee (UGC) visited the School and agreed that a new building should be erected with the UGC bearing the main part of the cost. Detailed planning for the Library component of the new building was vested in J. A. Boxhall, Estates Secretary, and B. C. Bloomfield, Deputy Librarian. For more than six years, they were responsible for consulting staff, library users and other interested parties on the design of the building. In particular, they were charged with liaising with Denys (later Sir Denys) Lasdun, the School's chosen architect, and his staff. Five key design principles shaped the design of the building:

1   That since the Library was in effect a series of libraries concerned with different regions and languages, the collections and facilities should be organized to mirror the academic and teaching structure of the School.

2   That in addition to general reading room and catalogue facilities that could be found in general academic libraries, there should be separate reference and seminar rooms with associated specialist staff located close to regional collections.

3   That the Library's collections should so far as possible be housed on open access shelves and that both the books and library staff should be easily accessible to all readers.

4   That the Library should become the heart of the School.

5   That the Library should not be 'imposing' or 'impressive' but welcoming, friendly and on a human scale.

A number of designs submitted had to be discarded because of external constraints. A tall Library building would be prohibitively expensive and unacceptable to the Royal Fine Art Commission which had ruled that no new building could exceed the height of the University's Senate House and, ideally, should not be higher than the roof of the British Museum's reading room. A Library with extensive underground bookstacks was also impractical given London's high water table. Finally, agreement was reached over the design of a relatively compact building serving as an extension to the original College building. The need for this building to house academic staff offices and teaching rooms as well as the new Library itself provided a number of dilemmas. Agreement could not be reached as to whether the Library should be located at the bottom of the building with academic accommodation above or vice versa. Finally, the architect proposed a design with the Library as an inner cone surrounded by an outer band of academic accommodation.

The final design provided for six floors of Library accommodation. The lower three floors are housed across the entire floor space available with the upper three floors arranged in tiers around an atrium. Although not universally admired – and initially regarded as the most expensive empty space in Bloomsbury – the interior layout offers one of the most spectacular sights in British academic libraries.

Work to clear the building site had begun in June 1969 and the building contracts were awarded in December of the same year. Following Philips's famous victory (described in Hugh Baker's chapter) over final attempts from pressure groups to halt building work due to concerns about preserving historic parts of Bloomsbury, the new building was finally completed and handed over to the School on 1 May

1973. The move into the new Library took some seven weeks during which time the Library maintained normal services to readers. The Library was formally opened on 5 October 1973 by the Chancellor, Her Majesty Queen Elizabeth the Queen Mother. As had been hoped during the planning phase, the Library was arranged around a number of regional collections: on the ground floor, South Asia, the Islamic Near East and non-Islamic Near East, on the first floor, Africa, on the second floor, South East Asia, China and Japan. Non-regional collections for the social sciences and Geography were housed on the lower ground floor and an Art collection, together with photographs, on the first floor. Reader spaces and accommodation for rare books and future collection development were housed on the upper two floors of the Library.

At the time of its opening, the Library provided accommodation for 550 readers and space for some one million volumes. A history of university library development in the UK at the time observed that 'on any reasonable calculation the School was freed from library accommodation problems until well into the 21st century'. But as has so often been the case with prophecies confidently advanced in the 1970s about the future of a British university, this forecast was be subjected to increasingly serious challenges by subsequent developments.

For a time the Library settled well into its new accommodation and its staff and users, particularly under the important guidance of the Library Committee, took advantage of Lasdun's design to adapt gradually to changing user demands, innovations in professional practice and expansions in collection development. By the 1990s, however, it was hardly possible to sustain this relatively comfortable regime. Pressures on space again began to be felt with increasing acuteness. Standing at 400,000 volumes when the new Library opened in 1973, the collection exceeded half a million by 1979 and reached the one million threshold by the mid-1990s.

Nor was this physical growth the only pressure to be faced. With the significantly increased number of taught course students which was such an important feature of the School's development at the time, a number of innovations had – not before time – to be put into place to serve a changing user population. In 1993 a Teaching Collection containing short-term loan copies of textbooks recommended on reading lists was established on the ground floor of the Library, while a few years later in 1998 the central Reading Hall on the first floor of the Library was relocated to allow the establishment of an on-line access computer suite for students. In addition to these enhanced provisions to address justifiable student expectations, which themselves impose an increasing strain upon the limited resources available to the Library, the needs of research users were addressed with the establishment in 1997 of a Special Collections reading room on the lower ground floor to provide high quality facilities to users of the Library's rapidly growing collection of archives, manuscripts and rare books.

Scope for significant development and enhancement came in 1999 by which time the Library's collection of nearly 1.2 million volumes far exceeded the space available in the Library. Consideration had been given to the establishment of an off-site remote store, but this was rejected on the grounds that the Library's particular strength was making the vast majority of its materials openly available to anyone entering it. An alternative strategy was proposed which involved relocating collections from the lower ground floor and installing mobile shelving on tramtracks. Engineering tests proved satisfactory and work was started in the summer of 2000. This provided some 6,680 linear metres of space, increasing the Library's storage capacity by 28 per cent on its initial capacity of 23,394 linear metres. The opportunity was taken at the same time to create a modern archives store, further details of which are given below at the end of this chapter. The relocation of collections within the Library to make best use of the new mobile shelving allowed the creation of much needed additional reader spaces although provision is still somewhat lower than is demanded by the School's current population. It is hoped that funding can be secured in the near future to allow the terraces on the north and east wings of the Library to be enclosed to provide further reader space.

A quarter century of heavy use had by this time visibly taken its toll on the physical fabric. The increasingly tired appearance of the Library was finally transformed through a refurbishment scheme which was started in 2000 and finally completed in 2002. Colour schemes and fittings selected in the late 1960s had come to look both out of date and rather worn, and funding was provided by external sources to allow for extensive refurbishment. Funding was also provided to create a new Issue Desk and entrance foyer which provide a more open and welcoming first impression to visitors than the more closed initial design which had been created to serve a much smaller user population.

Collections and staffing

Following the Hayter Report's recommendation that the Library be designated as a national resource, additional funding was provided to support collection development at a level beyond that normally seen in an institution the size of SOAS. It was the impact of this additional funding and subsequent financial settlements which enabled the Library's collections to grow at such a tremendous pace during the 1970s and 1980s.

The first formal statement of the Library's acquisitions policy was set out in 1965, in response to the Hayter Report. It has been revised on a number of subsequent occasions and a new version is in preparation intended to reflect the growing range of electronic resources which now sit alongside the traditional printed collections of the Library. Here it may be observed that the Library has always been keen to adopt and deploy new technology to improve services to users. The first significant automation project was the introduction of a computerized circulation system to control the issuing of books to users in 1974. In due course this system was succeeded first by Geac, then by Libertas, and more recently in 1999 by the Innopac Millenium system. This integrated system has allowed all of the Library's procedures to be automated together: circulation of books, their acquisition, ordering and cataloguing and the gathering of information about books recorded on course reading lists. Of particular significance to SOAS is the ability to record, retrieve and display information about books in a number of non-Roman scripts, including Chinese, Japanese, Arabic and Hebrew.

The national status of the SOAS Library and the wide renown of its collections are evidenced by the numbers of external users which it has always attracted. In a typical year the number of registered external members of the Library is broadly equivalent to those who are members of the School. In 2001 there were over 3,200 external members compared to some 3,700 staff and student borrowers, but these figures do not reflect the very large number of visitors entering on short-term passes, which annually exceeds 15,000.

The Library has also always sought to collaborate with other relevant libraries to provide the best possible support to its scholarly community. Collaboration, particularly to support the needs of taught course students, has chiefly been provided through reciprocal arrangements with libraries of other Colleges of the University of London and with the main University Library. Collaboration has worked effectively on a number of disciplinary fronts, ensuring that at least one copy of each important work in a given subject is available in one library within the University.

In the late 1990s, however, relations with the main University Library housed in Senate House became unfortunately strained by the changes in university funding which led to the introduction of charges for access to the University Library, meaning that the maintenance of universal access for SOAS staff and students to that important resource was now beyond the School's means. Student opposition to restricted access to their university library was so intense that the Students' Union voted to occupy the SOAS Library in late 1997. This occupation, which lasted for nearly two weeks, was one of three protests to disrupt the Library in recent years. Students had occupied the Library in January 1993 in protest at the inadequate supply of reading lists to the Library and the introduction of fines for books returned after their due date. A further student occupation in January 2000 in protest against the introduction by the government of student tuition fees did not directly affect the Library, although it was closed to readers for several days.

Meanwhile, collaboration on the national and international scene has allowed the Library to bring a wider range of research materials within easy reach of SOAS staff and students. Of particular significance is the formal collaborative agreement between SOAS and the British Library, which was signed in 1998. Although senior staff changes in both organizations have delayed significant progress, greatly improved reciprocal access arrangements and streamlined collecting procedures have already been achieved. A number of library groups with a regional focus, frequently with SOAS playing a leading role, have been established to ensure collaborative collection development, the production of guides for researchers, and cooperative staff training events. The first such grouping, SCOLMA (the Standing Conference on Library Materials on Africa), was established in 1962, and has been followed by organizations covering all other areas of the Library's regions of interest. Of particular significance is the work of the National Council on Orientalist Library Resources which acts as a coordinating body, bringing together all relevant regional groups.

The Library's early collections were enhanced significantly both by gifts and other donations and by trips to Asia and Africa by members of SOAS staff. Both of these important activities continue to this day and the quality of the Library's collections would be much poorer without them. Gifts to the Library in particular are of very great importance, whether of single volumes or of complete collections. Retiring academics, both from SOAS and other institutions, regularly present their personal libraries to the School, thus making available important works which are frequently out-of-print and difficult to acquire. Notable collections are mentioned later in this chapter, but of particular significance have been the bequest of books and papers on the Philippines by Ifor B. Powell, the Hardyman Collection on Madagascar and the Burma Campaign Memorial Library. These donations have been particularly important as they have helped to extend the Library's coverage across the School's vast regional remit. While the book buying tours mentioned elsewhere have helped to ensure coverage of the largest countries and regions, it is frequently through the presentation of materials gathered by private collectors and specialist groups that the Library is able to maintain coverage of other areas.

Many particular challenges have been presented to those responsible for developing the Library's collections in recent years. First amongst these has been the development of electronic information resources, which allow library users to access electronic versions of journal articles and other materials, frequently from internet connections around the world. By 2003, over 7,000 journal titles, many of them complete runs, were available in this way. This electronic approach to providing access to research materials builds on earlier purchases of significant collections assembled in the United States and elsewhere. The second and third challenges both relate principally to financial matters. Those familiar with the School will be aware that in recent years it has faced a number of financial pressures which have limited its ability to invest in its Library. These constraints have been compounded by inflation rates for books and scholarly journals which far exceed the inflation rates used to calculate grants to higher education institutions. Combined with a considerable growth in the volume of published scholarly output, the Library's current collecting levels are somewhat more modest than would be wished.

The changing character of the Library over the period has been both reflected in and shaped by the succession of its Librarians. Jim Pearson, who had been appointed Librarian in 1950 and who is remembered as the first compiler of the *Index Islamicus* which remains a key bibliographic resource for all involved with Islamic studies, moved into an academic role firstly as Senior Fellow and then as Professor of Bibliography with reference to Asia and Africa on 31 March 1972. He was succeeded as Librarian by Barry Bloomfield, who as Deputy Librarian had assumed much responsibility for planning the new Library building and who is also remembered as a bibliographer, not least for his bibliography of his friend the poet Philip Larkin. Bloomfield departed in 1978 to the India Office Library and was succeeded by V. T. H. Parry. A break with the all too notable SOAS tradition of appointing men to senior positions was then marked when Barbara Burton became Librarian in 1983. When she retired in 1992 the position was filled by Mary Auckland until her move to the new London Institute in 1998. Upon her departure the School decided to create the post of Librarian and Director of Information Services and Keith Webster of the University of Newcastle was appointed to this post in 1999. He moved into the new post of Director of Information Services and Strategy in 2002 but retained responsibility for the overall strategic direction and planning of the Library.

Under these leaders the Library's staff establishment increased considerably in the 1950s and 1960s but has remained broadly static in number over the past 30 years. The most significant change has been in the number of library staff, including those with regional language expertise, who possess professional qualifications in Library and Information Studies. The most distinctive feature of SOAS Library staffing structure is the regional and subject librarian grouping, comprising those who are specialists in the language and publications of a region of Asia or Africa. Their responsibilities embrace the selection and cataloguing of new library materials and the provision of reference and higher-level research support to students and staff. They collaborate closely with opposite numbers in other libraries around the world and many of them undertake book-buying tours in their regions of expertise.

Developments in library practice have brought about some change in the focus of regional and subject librarians. For example, catalogue records for the vast majority of books acquired by the Library are now available for transfer from major international databases of book records. The growth of disciplinary activity in the School, particularly in the social sciences, has resulted in overwhelming demand for English language publications about Asia and Africa, rather than literary and other works from the regions themselves. These changes have come at a time when changes in learning and teaching across higher education have increased demand for information skills training to be delivered by qualified librarians to students as part of their degree studies. Under the leadership of three Faculty Librarians, appointed in 2002 to liaise closely with the School's new academic faculties, regional and subject librarians have spent an increasing amount of their time working with groups of students and in preparing training materials and other library guides, as the Library, which has itself been transformed in so many ways, works to serve the needs of a very different institution from the SOAS of thirty years ago.

The archives

The first large archive to be received into the SOAS Library was that of the London Missionary Society (now the Council for World Mission) which arrived in 1973, following completion of the new Library building. Negotiations with the Council had begun during the 1970-71 session but it was quite impracticable for the School to absorb such a huge collection – nearly 2,000 archival boxes and 13,000 printed books from the old LMS Library – while existing Library accommodation was so limited. Following the Hayter Report and the delineation of the Library's 'national role' as a research resource for Asia and Africa, the Library had begun acquiring manuscript collections that would extend the range and the depth of the Library's collections. The Council's archive, placed in closed-access storage on the top floor of the new Library building and soon followed by other large archival collections, brought a new order of concerns into the Library. There were frequent references in the Library's *Annual Reports* at the time to the heavy use made of the archives. The report for 1974-75 presciently observed that the growth in the archive collections underlined 'the need for considering the development of a rare books and manuscript reading room where readers can be supervised with more care than is possible at present, and perhaps for increasing the air-conditioned area of the Library where such materials can be stored under suitable conditions'. It was, however, to be many years before those aspirations were fully met.

Archives and large manuscript collections continued to accumulate at SOAS throughout the rest of the 1970s and into the 1980s, and the overall strengths of the collections began to become clear. The size and range of the missionary holdings – over a million documents, thousands of photographs, and the contents of missionary libraries received along with the archives – made SOAS one of the largest and most important centres in the world for the study of the Western missionary movement in the eighteenth, nineteenth and twentieth centuries. Some chances were, regrettably, missed. Tentative overtures about housing archives of the Anglican missionary societies – the Church Missionary Society and the United Society for the Propagation of the Gospel – did not receive an encouraging response from the School and these significant collections went elsewhere. Nonetheless, a wide range of denominational and non-denominational missionary societies are represented in the missionary collections at SOAS. Records of the various missionary societies have been deliberately augmented by collections of the personal papers of missionaries since unofficial accounts are a highly valued complement to the official record.

138

'Missionary perils'

The Library has paid particular attention to building up archival and manuscript holdings relating to East Asia. During the 1960s and 1970s the papers of a number of former members of the Chinese Maritime Customs Service were deposited in the Library and similar collections continue to be received up to the present day. These include correspondence between the first Inspector-General of the Service, Sir Robert Hart and his London representative, J. D. Campbell, the papers of E. C. M. Bowra and his son C. A. Bowra, and the official papers of Sir Frederick Maze, Inspector-General from 1929 to 1943. A recent development has been the acquisition of collections of former members of the China Consular Service, including Sir Chaloner Alabaster, P. D. Coates, author of *China Consuls*, and Sir Alwyne Ogden. These range in time from the Opium Wars and the Taiping Rebellion to the Second World War and its aftermath. The papers of Sir John Pratt, also a member of the consular service, chiefly date from 1941: they document his campaigning activities against the Korean War and include letters from his younger brother, the horror movie star, Boris Karloff.

During the early 1980s the Library received a large consignment of the diaries, letters and papers of Sir Charles Addis, who went to China in 1883 with the Hongkong and Shanghai Bank, rose to become senior manager in its London Office and a director of the Bank of England, and who was in the inter-war years a leading financial adviser in London, Europe and America. The important archive of John Swire and Sons was acquired in 1975. The firm had been established in Liverpool in 1832, but its expansion into the Eastern markets came in the 1860s under John Samuel Swire. The company, known in East Asia as Butterfield and Swire, first dealt in textiles but subsequently switched to shipping, sugar refining and dockyards. Despite the loss of many records during the Second World War, the Swire archive is nonetheless an essential resource for business historians and has also been consulted by scholars investigating Anglo-Chinese relations.

Alongside these developments important collections of scholarly papers were acquired, either donated by SOAS scholars or by those connected with the School's activities. Among the most notable of these are the papers of Lieutenant-Colonel D. L. R. Lorimer of the Indian Political Service, recording pioneering work on the languages and peoples of the Karakoram region. He and his wife, Emily Overend Lorimer, journeyed to Hunza in the mid-1930s, creating a unique visual record in both film and still photography of the people and customs of that remote region which still attracts considerable interest. Another scholar who has left an important visual and documentary resource, particularly on the tribal societies of northeast and central India, is Professor Christoph von Fürer-Haimendorf, whose work is referred to in several other contributions to this volume. Sadly, some scholars are far less well represented. All that remains of the papers of Alice Werner (1859-1935) who taught African languages in the School from 1917 to 1929 are a handful of documents and postcards.

In 1983 an important development took place when an Advisory Sub-Committee on Archives was inaugurated. This body, which has helped to secure the place of the archives within the School through both formal and informal links, has met once or twice a year ever since to advise the Archivist on collecting policy and to provide a forum for the discussion of issues relating to the development of the archives. The Sub-Committee's brief, wider than those of the other Library Advisory Sub-Committees, was 'to keep under review the policy of acquisition, maintenance and use of archives'. In practice, the main activity of the Sub-Committee has been to advise on acquisition policy. A Statement of Collecting Policy was drawn up which, in essentials, has changed very little over the years. The main features of this policy were to 'acquire archives, manuscripts and other primary source materials of research value for Asian and African studies', especially within the categories of (1) missionaries, missionary organizations and religious groups; (2) business organizations and individuals involved in business; (3) humanitarian organizations and political non-government groups; and (4) individuals whose life or work has been of special significance to the study of Africa and Asia.

By the 2000-01 session, there were more than 4,000 linear metres of archives, manuscripts and other special materials in SOAS Library, including some 12,000 boxes and volumes of archives and manuscript collections and 3,000 individual manuscripts. Most collections offered have been accepted, though the Sub-Committee has turned away some which it felt did not meet its criteria. It has discouraged would-be depositors from depositing materials not yet open to consultation and has required them to take steps to organize and list materials before transfer takes place. Ownership of many of the larger archives has been retained by the depositing organizations and this has had significant consequences as far as the administration of the collections is concerned, particularly in copyright matters, but also in terms of financing cataloguing and preservation.

Administering large archival collections was, by the mid-1980s, proving proble-matic. The Library made its first appointment to an archives post in 1978 but it was becoming clear, less than ten years further on, that one member of staff, however energetic and well-motivated, could not do all that was necessary to sort, arrange and catalogue materials and be available to answer letters, help researchers, preserve and promote the collections, and carry out other Library duties. Cataloguing, in particular, suffered. A daunting stack of uncatalogued materials was accumulating on the top floor of the Library in cartons, suitcases, and piles which tended to topple over and merge despite valiant efforts to keep them apart. Action was urgently needed, and in 1989, with letters of support from academics, a successful application was made to the Leverhulme Trust to fund a three-year project to catalogue thirty to forty manuscript collections relating to the history of various parts of Africa, Asia and Oceania. Sufficient funding was provided to do all that was wished for, and slightly more. By the end of 1993 forty collections had been sorted, boxed, and fully catalogued enabling the first consolidated and illustrated *Guide to Archives and Manuscript Collections in the Library* to appear in the following year, funded by a timely grant from John Swire & Sons.

The major development of the archives at SOAS came during the second half of the 1990s. A wish list had been drawn up by the Archivist, in consultation with the Librarian and the Advisory Sub-Committee, then chaired by David Anderson of the History Department. Heading the list was the need to improve security and support for the consultation of archives, manuscripts and rare books. With greatly increased numbers of undergraduates, use of the main reading room, where the Teaching Collection was also housed, had increased dramatically. Archives users had, almost literally, to fight for reader space. Nor were the overworked staff in the reading room able to provide anything like the scrutiny such valuable materials required. Losses were inevitable and a number, regrettably, did take place. In 1993 a valuable Malay manuscript went missing, following its consultation in the main reading room. The fact that it turned up a year later at the bottom of the lift-shaft to which it had doubtless tumbled from a book trolley did not diminish the argument for a new reading room. A dedicated reading room for the consultation of the Library's rare and unique materials had now become imperative.

The Library's opportunity came in 1994, when a new funding programme to support specialized research collections in the humanities was announced by the higher education funding bodies for England, Scotland, Wales and Northern Ireland. Recurring funding was to be made available to projects which enhanced access to collections through publicity, development of the collections, or support for user-related services. SOAS was successful in securing an award of £247,000 over four years: this not only paid for the construction and equipping of a dedicated reading room but also staffed it until 1998. The new Special Collections reading room, with seats for fifteen researchers, bookcases for reference materials, two user computers, a supervisor's desk, an overnight store, and adjacent office space, opened to readers in January 1997 and was officially opened by Sir Brian Follett, Chairman of the Libraries Review, a few months later. The new reading room has proved popular with researchers, as can be seen from the following table:

	1998-1999	1999-2000	2000-2001	2001-2002
Number of readers	2,093	2,177	2,174	2,140
Items requisitioned	3,968	4,086	3,371	4,032

Several other cataloguing projects were successfully accomplished during the same period with HEFCE funding, first under its non-recurrent funding programme for Specialized Research Collections in the Humanities programme in 1994-95 and, from 1999-2000, under the Research Support Libraries Programme: in all, SOAS Archives and Manuscripts Division has received in excess of £530,000 from these programmes. The first programme funded the purchase of a new automated cataloguing system CAIRS in 1996. Records created under the Leverhulme project were successfully imported into the new system though older finding aids have to be keyed in – a daunting task for the future. On-line catalogues were created for both the Council for World Mission Library and the Methodist Missionary Society, greatly improving access to these two heavily used collections. In 2000 a start was made with arranging and cataloguing the very large collections of missionary photographs, numbering around 35,000 images, which had been received along with the archives but had remained almost totally unlisted. A further important funding development came in 1998 when the Council for World Mission generously agreed to endow its collections at SOAS and to begin a 'programme of co-operation and collaboration to ensure the physical survival of the CWM archive and library and provide for their professional management'. Under the terms of the endowment a new and permanent post of Assistant Archivist was established with special responsibility for the administration and cataloguing of the CWM Archive. Following this precedent, the Methodist Church offered, in 2001 to support a part-time Archivist to curate and catalogue the archive of the Methodist Missionary Society. It is hoped that similar collaborative relationships with other major depositors will ensure that all the SOAS archives can be preserved and catalogued to the highest possible standards.

For some years the conditions in which the School's archives, manuscripts and rare books were housed had been causing concern. Though, on the whole, securely stored on the top floor of the Library, the physical environment was wholly unsuited for the storage of valuable and fragile materials. At the same time the Library was running out of space. In 1999 the new Librarian and Director of Information Services, Keith Webster, proposed that the contents of the top two floors of the Library should be decanted into compact mobile storage on Level F (the basement floor) of the Library, releasing much-needed space for the Library's book collections. This arrangement also meant that the Library's rare materials could be brought into an area adjacent to the newly built Special Collections reading room. It was decided to take advantage of the imminent publication of revised standards for archival storage to make the new store as fully compliant as possible with the latest standards. The necessary works were carried out in the summer and autumn of 2000 and the bulk of the archives, manuscripts and rare books collections were moved into the new store in February 2001. Archive staff were delighted with such a state-of-the art store, though it was noted that little space was available for future growth and development.

The new archives store

It might be asked what the importance is of these collections to the School and to the national and international research community. The archival collections are among the largest in a higher educational institution in London and are among those most frequently consulted. Whereas archive reading rooms in other London colleges commonly have four or five persons a day consulting manuscript collections, the average number of daily visitors to the SOAS Library's Special Collections reading room is nine, rising to twelve in the summer months. Most users are from outside the School, though the percentage of SOAS users has risen slightly in recent years. The missionary archives, particularly those of the Council for World Mission, the Methodist Missionary Society and the China Inland Mission continue to attract scholars from around the world. A number of events years have shown, too, how these materials can be used as showpieces for the School. David Arnold, then Chair of the Archives Sub-Committee, and the Archivist, Rosemary Seton, organized a highly successful Missionary Archives Workshop at the School in 1992 which drew more than a hundred participants (the papers were published in 1996, in a volume edited by Robert Bickers and Rosemary Seton entitled *Missionary Encounters: Sources and Issues*). A special lecture given by Professor Andrew Porter of King's College, London, on 'The Council for World Mission and its Archival Legacy' was given in March 1999 to commemorate the inauguration of the CWM endowment and it, too, attracted an excellent audience. It is intended to follow up Professor Porter's lecture with another special lecture in the near future. Other development plans include participation in a Getty-funded project to digitize many of the missionary photographs held in the archives and plans are afoot to organize a major missionary exhibition in the Brunei Gallery.

The Archives and Manuscripts Division is now well placed and equipped to play a much fuller role in the School than formerly. We can be justly proud of our archive accommodation, we have extremely good consultation facilities and, best of all, we have a committed and well-motivated team of staff, a number of whom have professional archive qualifications and/or research and teaching experience. We are used to introducing groups of students and other visitors to our collections and to teaching them to appreciate and evaluate the raw materials of scholarship and research. Ironically enough however, we are more likely to be imparting these skills to external students and groups of visitors than to the School's own students. Discussions are in train with the School's recently appointed Curriculum Advisor to incorporate our skills and services into future learning and teaching programmes.

Finally, mention should be made of the School's own written and printed records, the deficiencies of which have been painfully apparent to those of us engaged in compiling this history. Lord Briggs, writing recently remarked that universities as institutions 'must safeguard, assemble and catalogue their own archives'. With the University of Sussex specifically in mind, he continued, 'just because the University... is young it has a special responsibility as the first of the new universities to ensure that it discharges its responsibility efficiently and imaginatively'. If this is true of a new University like Sussex, founded in the 1960s, how much more true it must be of an institution founded as long ago as 1916, particularly one of such rare and distinctive traditions, whose history deserves to be told and whose archival legacy requires due ordering and preservation.

8

The SOAS estate

Frank Dabell

Pressures and constraints

In most organizations the need for additional buildings is usually driven by the need for additional space, which in turn is almost always driven by numbers. In universities, the impetus comes primarily from an increase in staff and student numbers, the number of books and other material needed, and the number and type of facilities required. In recent years, technology has played a role in determining what types of facilities are required and the rapid expansion in IT facilities for students in the 1990s is a good example of how technology can impact upon space needs.

The higher education sector has changed considerably since the end of the Second World War, shaped largely by government policy and priorities. At the end of the war, with the exception of teacher training, higher education, and universities in particular, were not an immediate priority. For most institutions, the 1950s were a period of quiet retrenchment. The realization that the post-war economy needed more highly trained and skilled graduates saw a shift in government thinking and policy, which was exemplified by the publication of the Robbins Report in 1963, by the creation of new universities in the 1960s and the expansion of existing institutions. For a period of almost fifteen years, the higher education sector developed and grew as successive governments sought to expand the number of undergraduate and postgraduate students. Most of the expansion was achieved through increases in institutions' recurrent grants and the injection of major capital funding. However, in the late 1970s there was a considerable slowdown in capital resources made available to universities and in 1981 there was a major shift in the way in which government was prepared to fund higher education. With the government committed to bringing public spending under control, higher education suffered with many other services. There was a major cut in funding in real terms and temporarily these cuts caused a curtailment in the expansion of the sector, particularly amongst the so-called pre-1992 universities of which SOAS is one. The reduction in funding was to be maintained for nearly twenty years as successive governments regarded the sector as a relatively low priority.

Inevitably, government policy about student numbers changed again in the late 1980s (with the 1987 White Paper *Higher Education: Meeting the Challenge*), as there was a growing recognition that there was a need for more graduates, particularly in science and engineering. Government was prepared to fund this expansion by providing additional resources for teaching expanded undergraduate numbers. However, there was no large injection of capital to provide infrastructure, as had been the case in the 1960s and early 1970s. Many commentators have observed that this shift in government policy created a scramble for additional student numbers, as Vice-Chancellors realized that the expansion could not continue indefinitely given the far-reaching implications for the public purse. Ironically, much of the expansion occurred in subjects other than science and technology and in that sense government policy was frustrated. It was inevitable that this expansion of student numbers would eventually be curtailed and this occurred in 1994 with the introduction of the maximum aggregate student number, known in the sector as the 'MASN'. This capped the number of students institutions could recruit by penalizing those that exceeded these targets. This constraint continued until 2002 when the policy was relaxed to allow further expansion of undergraduate numbers.

Unfortunately, the introduction of the MASN was also accompanied by a deliberate policy of squeezing the unit of resource for teaching, effectively pulling back some of the funds that had been given to pay for the additional student numbers. This created financial instability in many institutions, including SOAS. The consequence was that there was a need to continue the expansion to underwrite operating costs and this could only be achieved at SOAS and elsewhere through the growth of postgraduate student numbers or non-degree programmes. As the graph on p.4 shows, between 1987 and 1992 undergraduate numbers rose significantly but were effectively stable for the remainder of the 1990s. Postgraduate student numbers, on the other hand, especially Masters numbers, continued to expand throughout the same period. By the early 1990s, the pressure on the SOAS estate caused by increased student numbers was acute and action had to be taken to acquire additional premises. The pressure was to continue throughout the 1990s.

In his account of the early history of the School (summarized in Chapter Two of this volume), Sir Cyril Philips argued that by 1967 the School had put itself in a position where it could offer a comprehensive, attractive and relevant range of courses. The academic changes that he had made, together with the construction of a new Library and academic facility, would, he claimed, allow the School to grow to 1,200 to 1,500 students, of which he envisaged a high proportion would be graduates. In fact, it took much longer than Sir Cyril had envisaged to reach these student numbers. It was only in 1990 that the lower figure was reached, with the higher one being achieved the following year. Hence, by 1991 SOAS had finally used up any spare capacity for academic activity created by what is now known as the Philips building, which had been completed in 1974. Looking back, it is easy to see that the School was set for a period of considerable growth. There had been a doubling of the student population in the period 1989-93 and numbers increased by a further 50 percent between 1993 and 1999. The initial growth was at the undergraduate level but this shifted to postgraduate and non-degree programmes during the late 1990s. By 2002, total student numbers had risen to above 3,500.

The Brunei Gallery

Coping with this growth created a frenetic phase in the development of the SOAS estate. With capital grants from the then Universities Funding Council (UFC) being scaled down significantly, it was clear that all new premises would have to be funded in part by the School or from benefactions made to the School. During 1991, two ideas began to evolve. The first was to construct an infill block at basement, ground and first floor levels on the northern elevation of the original College Building. The second was the proposal to construct an Islamic Art Centre on land to be acquired from the University of London, which would comprise a teaching block and an art gallery. It was hoped that this could be funded from a benefaction. The School was most fortunate that, by the summer of 1991, His Royal Highness the Sultan of Brunei had agreed to donate £10 million for the new building. In recognition of this magnificent gift it was agreed that the building should be named after the benefactor and the name was changed to the Brunei Gallery.

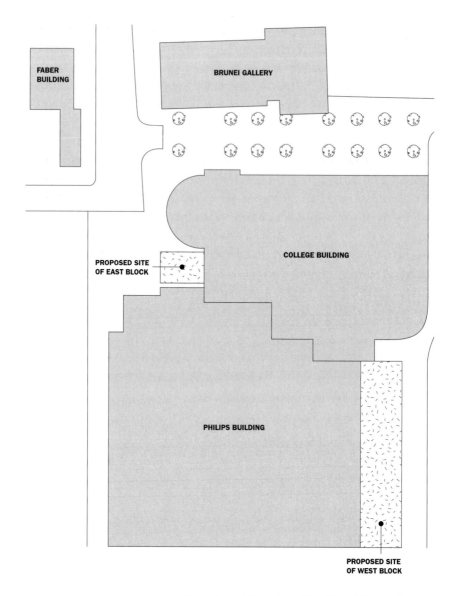

Lower ground floor plan of the Russell Square Campus

AHP Architects were instructed to design the infill block and an application was made in February 1992 to the UFC for part-funding of a minor capital project. By May 1992, the UFC had awarded the School a total of £637,000 out of a total project cost estimated at £1.39 million. By late 1992, planning approval had been achieved and Jarvis and Sons were appointed as the contractors. In spite of problems of access to the site and a tight construction period, the works were completed in the summer of 1993 and the building was available for occupation in early September. The building was intended to house the Registry and the Finance Departments. Meanwhile, the Brunei Gallery project was progressing with a planning application being made by Nicholas Hare Architects, acting for the Sultan, to the London Borough of Camden in December 1992. A start on site was made in the summer of 1993 and the building was completed in July 1995 and formally opened by the Chancellor of the University of London, HRH the Princess Royal on 22 November 1995. On the completion of the Brunei Gallery, the road between the original College Building and the new Brunei Gallery was pedestrianized and landscaped. At a stroke, visitors to SOAS were afforded a safer passage and, for the first time, the SOAS community enjoyed the benefit of a pleasant external environment.

The planning and construction of the Brunei Gallery was not achieved without some difficulties. In seeking planning consent for the Gallery, the School and the University of London overlooked a restrictive covenant in the original purchase contract when the land was acquired from the Russell family. The covenant required the University of London to consult with the Russell family before any new buildings were constructed. The consequence of this oversight was that on the eastern façade there is a singular plaque inscribed as follows:

> *The University of London hereby records its sincere apologies that the plans of this building were settled without due consultation with the Russell family and their Trustees and therefore without their approval of its design.*

The complexity of the building's design also resulted in an overrun in terms of cost and time with the building being commissioned almost a year late. However, it is a testament to Nicholas Hare's design that in 1998 the building was recognized as worthy of a Civic Trust Award. Today, the two plaques sit together side by side, in incongruous company with one other, on the eastern façade of the Brunei building, where a steady stream of tourists read and photograph them.

To buy time until the Brunei Gallery was opened, it proved necessary for the School to acquire three properties in Bloomsbury on a leasehold basis. 30 Russell Square was taken on a short lease from the University in 1991, 4 Gower Street was leased from the University in 1992 and 46/47 Russell Square from the Bedford Estate in September 1993. The lease on 30 Russell Square was surrendered in 1995 once the Brunei Gallery had been completed but it proved impossible to release the other premises as originally planned. The leases at 30 and 46/47 Russell Square were symbolically important as for the first time two academic departments (Art and Archaeology and Law respectively) were moved out of the School's main Bloomsbury premises. By 1994, it had become clear that even with the opening of the Brunei Gallery, the School would have insufficient space to meet the needs of its growing population. It was a moment of good fortune in the School's history that at that time the University decided to release 23/24 Russell Square, a Victorian property adjacent to the School's main premises. Only a few months earlier, the School's Governing Body had decided as a matter of policy that in future, wherever possible, the School should invest in its estate and occupy space on a freehold or near freehold basis. As a result, 23/24 Russell Square was purchased on a 99-year lease from the University and refurbished to be used as an office and teaching block at a total cost of £2.25 million. The School's surveyors, Tuffin Ferraby & Taylor, designed and managed the contract to time and on budget and the building opened in the summer of 1995. The building was named after one of the former early occupants, the publishers Faber & Faber, although it is particularly known (in certain quarters) for being the workplace for many years of that firm's most famous employee, the poet T. S. Eliot.

The SOAS student residences

During 1993-94, it became clear that the School required considerable expertise to assist in the management and development of the growing SOAS estate. This was reinforced by the Higher Education Funding Council for England (HEFCE) requiring institutions to submit 'estate strategies' as part of their Corporate Plans. As a result, an Estate Sub-Committee of the Finance and General Purposes Committee was created and SOAS was fortunate to attract Bryan Jefferson as the first Chair of the Committee. An architect himself, Jefferson had formerly been the head of the Public Services Agency and had assisted the School in the development of the Brunei Gallery. It was under his able stewardship that the Committee began to address the issue of student residences. Although the School had occasionally thought about the development of student residential accommodation, 1994-95 was the first time when there was any systematic thought given to the issue. Until that time, SOAS students had either had to fend for themselves or hope that they could obtain a place in the University of London Intercollegiate Halls. With growing realization in the School that there would need to be a concerted effort to expand student numbers, there was also increasing recognition that SOAS would need to offer students similar facilities to those provided by local competitors, such as University College London (UCL) and the London School of Economics (LSE). Most critically, this required the offer of student residential places to first-year undergraduate and postgraduate students.

In convincing the School's Governing Body that acquiring residences was essential, the Estate Sub-Committee also took a number of important supplementary decisions. The first was that ideally the residences should be within walking distance of the School, defined as a radius of one mile. Secondly, it was agreed that SOAS should build residences to a high standard, mirroring the small number of residences that had been built by our competitors in the early 1990s with en suite facilities. Following much discussion, it was decided that the residences should take the form of residential flats, comprising five or six en suite bedrooms with a kitchen/dining facility. Thirdly, it was recognized that the residences had to be self-financing and had to be purchased with loan financing obtained in the market place. Fourthly, to minimize risk, it was agreed that residences should be built on a 'design and build' basis, transferring the majority of the financial risk to the contractor. During 1994, the then College Secretary, Frank Dabell, assembled a professional team that was prepared to work on a speculative basis towards the achievement of the purchase of land and its development for student residences. This professional team was to provide the cornerstone for all the major projects that the School was to undertake in the following six years and included the London based architects T P Bennett and the developers R & M Projects Ltd.

By the end of 1994 a suitable site had been identified on Pentonville Road. It was owned by the National Westminster Bank but was surplus to their requirements. With their permission, planning consent for the development of 505 student residential places was sought from the London Borough of Islington. This planning application was pursued successfully by T. P. Bennett Architects and following the usual tendering procedures, Wimpey Construction Ltd were appointed as contractors and began work on site in the summer of 1995. The project proceeded to time and to budget (£11.6 million) and the residence opened for the new intake of students in September 1996. Following an internal consultation exercise, it was agreed that the residence should be known as Dinwiddy House in honour of Caroline Dinwiddy, a senior lecturer in economics, who had been tragically killed in December 1994 in a traffic accident while serving as the Dean of Undergraduate Studies. Given the enthusiasm with which she taught successive generations of students and the significant contribution she made to their welfare, it was an appropriate and welcome decision.

Even before Dinwiddy House opened, it became clear that the continued expansion of the School would require further residential places and the search for suitable sites continued. By good fortune, the professional team identified a site within 400 metres of Dinwiddy House on Penton Rise. The site was owned by Glynwed International Plc, a well-known engineering company, who agreed to sell the land by private treaty. After careful consideration, it was agreed that the School should not proceed to develop the whole site for its own purposes. The site was of sufficient size to provide in excess of 400 residential places in two major residential blocks. As it was known that the neighbouring college, UCL, was in the market for additional student residences, they were invited to become a partner in the scheme. SOAS purchased the land from Glynwed Properties Ltd in January 1997 and sold on a portion of the site to UCL. Berkeley College Homes were appointed as contractors by both SOAS and UCL and construction began in April 1997: the work was completed in the summer of 1998 in time for the new session. At SOAS, it was agreed to name this new residence, to be used for postgraduate students, after Paul Robeson the black American singer who had briefly studied at SOAS in the 1930s. UCL opted to name their residence James Lighthill House after a former Provost of the College. Robeson House provided SOAS with a much needed additional 280 rooms.

By the time that the School made its annual report to HEFCE in 1995, it had become clear that the financial forecasts to 2000 would require total student numbers to increase to over 2,500 if the School was to continue to flourish. In order to address the issue of acquiring space for this growth, the Estate Sub-Committee made two important decisions: firstly, to investigate whether additional space could be created around the main buildings at Russell Square; and, secondly, to employ expert help in carrying out this investigation. These decisions resulted in the architects John McAslan & Partners (JMP) being appointed in 1996 to develop what was to become the Campus Development Plan. Following a number of interim reports, the School finally gave permission to JMP to make a planning application to the London Borough of Camden in July 1999. The proposed JMP scheme was ingenious in that it sought to take advantage of what little land the School held on a long lease from the University adjoining the College and Philips Buildings. There were three main elements to the Plan. The first was a small teaching block to be built on the eastern elevation between the College and the Philips Buildings. It was hoped that this new teaching block, given the temporary name of 'the East Block', would also provide additional lifts to improve vertical movement in the main buildings, an urgent priority given the considerable increase in internal traffic. The second element was to enclose the northern terrace of the Philips Building, expanding the envelope of the Library at first floor level. The third and final element was a proposal to build a major academic facility on land adjacent to the western elevation of the Philips Building facing Birkbeck College.

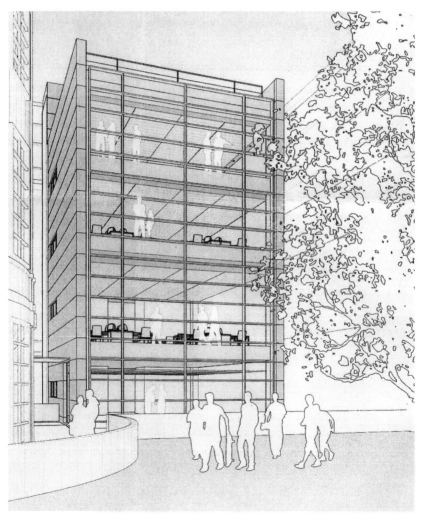

Architect's drawing of the East Block

155

It was always recognized that obtaining planning permission would be difficult given the proximity of two Grade II listed buildings and the inevitable interest of two local interest groups, the Twentieth Century Society and the Bloomsbury Conservation Society. It was also necessary to consult with the Philips Building architect, Sir Denys Lasdun, also the architect of the South Bank complex, as it was well known that he had strong views about any modifications to his buildings. However, all of this was successfully navigated and planning permission for the East and West Blocks was granted by Camden on 10 July 2000. It seemed that the problem of additional space could be overcome on the Russell Square site and the attention of all those concerned shifted to identifying sources of funding.

It was, however, immediately recognized that there was little possibility of capital funding from HEFCE and that the School's own ability to borrow enough funds had been compromised by the capital raised in the markets for 23/24 Russell Square, Dinwiddy House and Paul Robeson House. Action was needed to free the School from its financial constraints and the solution identified was both innovative and a university sector leader. In a relatively small institution, the problem of managing the projects for the construction of Dinwiddy and Paul Robeson Houses had proved time-consuming. It had also become necessary to set up management systems to deal with the day-to-day management of the residences, their maintenance and the collection of student rents. With the growing complexity and bureaucracy of higher education management, this proved to be an unwelcome distraction from the School's core activities. The idea evolved as to whether it would be possible for the School to continue to enjoy the benefit of the student residences without the headache of owning and managing them. If this could be achieved much-needed capital would be released.

It was here that SOAS benefited greatly from the London property market boom of the late 1990s. The site and construction costs of both residences were relatively modest compared to the 1999 prices. At the same time, because all institutions in London were experiencing the need to build additional residences, rental levels for high quality accommodation had risen sharply. Although the SOAS rentals were below those of our immediate competitors, there was adequate income from the residences for them to command a much higher value than they had originally cost. To test this idea it was agreed that Dinwiddy House should be placed on the market on a tendering basis to see if anyone would purchase the freehold, subject to the condition that they managed the residences as SOAS residences providing accommodation for a guaranteed period at a guaranteed price to SOAS students.

In the event, the market proved to be receptive to the idea and a major London Housing Association, Shaftesbury, successfully bid for and acquired Dinwiddy House in December 1999, followed by Paul Robeson House in August 2000. This allowed SOAS to clear its loan facilities and to make major capital gains while freeing up considerable management time. It is hardly surprising that many other institutions in the sector have since sought to enter into similar arrangements.

In taking the decision to dispose of the freeholds of the two student residences, the Governing Body also resolved that the funds raised would be used for infrastructure projects to invest in the School's future. The funding raised was to be invested in a number of academic initiatives, a new telephone exchange, an upgrade of the School's IT network and new fire-alarm systems. It was also anticipated that funds would be available for future building projects.

Towards a second campus

Following the granting of planning permission for the two main elements of the Campus Development Plan, a series of initiatives was put in hand to rationalize the School's estate. The first was the acquisition on a short lease of space in Lynton House in Tavistock Square to provide temporary accommodation for some administrative functions, which were to be decanted from the College Buildings. The second was that it was also agreed that a start should be made in the summer of 2000 on the construction of the East Block. It was hoped that this would enable the release of the lease of 46/47 Russell Square on which the School had an option to break in October 2001. Sadly, 46/47 Russell Square had never provided ideal academic accommodation and with the property boom continuing, rental levels were set to rise significantly. It was in the School's interest to free itself from these expensive leasehold premises.

There was a final (and, in some quarters, sensitive) issue to be overcome before the East Block could be constructed: the SOAS squash courts. The two courts occupied part of the site on which the East Block was to be built. These were in poor condition as a result of some years of neglect but the prospect of their demolition soon elevated them to an iconic status. It was argued that they made a major contribution to the health and well-being of the School. Fortunately, this myth fell to earth with a bump when it was discovered that over 80 percent of those using the courts were from other institutions. Resistance rapidly crumbled.

It was, then, with some optimism that the summer of 2000 saw the start on site by the contractors, Mansell Construction, who had been appointed following a tendering exercise by John McAslan & Partners. However, the project was beset with problems, partly caused by planning issues and partly by the difficulty of working in such a confined site. Unfortunately, worse was to follow at the start of the session in the autumn of 2000. While it is true that the need for more space is driven by numbers, it is equally true that the need for circulation space increases as the number of people moving around the buildings increase. This had been partly recognized in that the design of the East Block was to provide two additional lifts to increase vertical movement in the College and Philips Buildings. What had not been anticipated was that a further increase in student numbers in September 2000 would cause the high level of congestion experienced, particularly at the time of the first fire evacuation drill. When the bells rang, everyone moved quickly to the exits only to come to a halt for several minutes as the congestion on the main stairwells made further progress impossible. Urgent action had to be taken as it was clear that total student numbers now using the main buildings had to be reduced. As expanding student numbers on site was no longer an option, and with there being no prospect of acquiring significant additional accommodation in the immediate Bloomsbury area, it became evident that the School would have to think in terms of a second campus.

Earlier that summer, School officers had been alerted to the possibility that a major school building, adjacent to Paul Robeson House, might come on to the market. The main building had been erected as an Edwardian school and was a solid and impressive four-storey building. It had originally been called the Sir Philip Magnus Secondary School. In more recent years it had become a satellite building for a local further education college, Kingsway College. However, it had become surplus to requirements of the college and had been sold to a developer in 1999. Fortunately for SOAS, the Islington planners had taken a less than favourable view of the various planning applications that had been made to them by the developer. What had been envisaged had been the demolition of the school building and the use of the site for a hotel. The Borough planning officials expressed a strong desire to maintain an education use on the site and were very receptive to an approach from the School to hold firm on this issue. Once the planning constraints became clear the developer became receptive to selling the building. Its value remained affordable to SOAS because of the restrictive education planning use.

It was a stroke of good fortune in timing that was to provide SOAS with the opportunity to create a second campus on the site within a minute's walk of both the School's residences and within a mile of Russell Square. Professor Philip Stott, a geographer who was to become the first Dean of the School's second campus, observed that in acquiring the site SOAS had the opportunity to make it a vibrant home for many students, bringing life and learning back to an ever-changing area of London. Largely through the School's own effort and initiative, the southwest corner of Islington was to be regenerated with the construction of two student residences followed by the development of a second SOAS campus.

The freehold of the building was acquired in November 2000 and an immediate planning application was made to allow for the creation of four lift-shafts and thus provide for the necessary access to the four-storey building. Mansell Construction were awarded the contract and began on site on 3 January 2001. Work had to be completed by August to allow the building to be commissioned in time for the start of the 2001-02 academic session. The timetable was daunting. It was a remarkable achievement of all of those involved that the project ran to time and to budget. During the planning stages of the development of the second campus, it became obvious that there would be a need to identify both campuses by name. The newly acquired building was accessed through Vernon Square and it soon became evident that both campuses could be associated with a London square. There was general approval for the idea of renaming the Bloomsbury complex as the 'Russell Square' campus and designating the new campus as 'Vernon Square'. It is a testament to the immense effort made by the project leaders, Professor Philip Stott and the Deputy Secretary, Geraldine Hennelly, that the project was completed successfully, opening in time for the 2001-02 session.

The School's second campus was formally opened by the Chancellor of the University of London, HRH the Princess Royal, on 18 October 2001. With the opening occurring at a time when the events of 11 September 2001 in New York and Washington were still in everyone's mind, the Chancellor aptly commented upon the importance of SOAS's role in promoting an understanding of the world's regions.

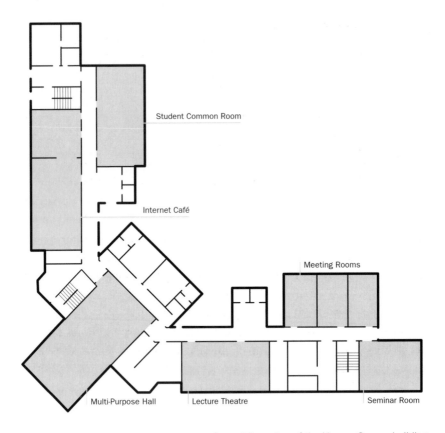

Ground floor plan of the Vernon Square building

In planning for the second campus, account had to be taken of the way in which teaching was conducted in the School and the facilities that were to be made available at Vernon Square. As a former Edwardian school building, there were many large classrooms and it was agreed at the outset that the building would be used to house Student Services, the Registry and the Finance Department as well as providing many new classrooms and lecture theatres and other necessary student facilities. It was hoped for the future that the Vernon Square campus could be further developed to provide office accommodation that might at some point house several of the School's academic activities. In the short term, a significant proportion of the School's undergraduate and postgraduate teaching was shifted from Russell Square to Vernon Square. The problem of congestion at Russell Square, which had at one time threatened to overwhelm the old SOAS buildings, had effectively been solved.

Further campus developments

The Vernon Square campus has become a major, and increasingly familiar, feature of the new SOAS. But other (and in some regards no less vital) aspects of the School's estate remain less well known. During the same period as the major expansion of the SOAS estate in the second half of the 1990s, SOAS became involved in a major scheme to deliver cost-effective heat and power to its main premises in Russell Square. In 1995, the School was supplied with heat from two district heating systems. The first dated back to the 1940s and served Birkbeck College, the original SOAS main building, the Warburg Institute and the University of London Union. The second was constructed as part of the Philips Building and supplied that building, together with the Institute of Advanced Legal Studies, the Institute of Education and a small part of UCL. In addition, there was a local electricity distribution system, which served approximately one half of these buildings. This existing infrastructure allowed the possibility that there could be a cost-effective introduction of a Combined Heat and Power (CHP) scheme. As a result, Frank Dabell convinced the other local institutions that there was value in pursuing the feasibility of a CHP scheme and within a relatively short period of time this feasibility was confirmed. A consortium of local colleges was created with the purpose of procuring heat and power for its members at the lowest overall cost, subject to adequate safeguards in respect of service level provisions and compliance with all relevant legislation. Within weeks the SOAS community had associated the CHP scheme with the export of 'hot air': the label has stuck.

It was at about the same time that the government was pushing the private finance initiative (PFI) and HEFCE soon announced a pathfinder project scheme, whereby suitable schemes would be supported in respect of professional fees. Hence, the Bloomsbury Combined Heat and Power Consortium (BCHPC) was formed and became a pathfinder project. The process was time-consuming and complex: starting with an invitation to tender in August 1996, it took until June 1998 to establish the preferred bidder and until January 2000 for Utilicom to be appointed as the successful contractor. It was not until September 2000 that the CHP engines had been delivered on site and been fully commissioned. The scheme proved to be highly successful with significant reductions in utility charges being achieved. In addition, CHP has the benefit of being more environmentally friendly than major power stations and, as a consequence, is encouraged by government by not being subject to an environmental surcharge. Hence, BCHPC members not only enjoyed the benefit of a reduction in existing costs but also avoided the additional cost of the levy. A further benefit is that the colleges will reduce their costs, as additional third-party users are connected to the scheme. This is possible because the SOAS boiler house has sufficient capacity for the scheme to be expanded significantly and the first third-party load, the London School of Hygiene and Tropical Medicine, was connected in 2001.

By 1999, it had been recognized that the Library would soon be at capacity, with only enough free shelving to house two or three more years' purchases. Urgent action was necessary. It was hoped that eventually the northern terrace element of the Campus Development Plan would provide additional reader facilities but the structure was insufficiently robust for this space to be used for book storage. Early investigations into the strength of the basement floor of the Library building had indicated that this area too could not be used for long-term book storage of those sections of the School's collections that were less frequently used. As a consequence, attention shifted to looking to house some of the School's collections offsite, possibly in an appropriate form of warehousing on an industrial estate in one of the less expensive suburbs of London. It seemed that history had come full circle, as this type of offsite provision had been necessary when the School began to outgrow its original College Building thirty-five years earlier and space had been rented from Royal Holloway College in Egham.

The arrival in 1999 of a new Librarian and Director of Information Services, Keith Webster, caused a reappraisal of the possibility of utilizing the basement for long-term storage. For reasons best known to structural engineers, a revised opinion was given and work was put in hand in 2000 to prepare a feasibility study for placing moveable long-term library storage shelving into the basement. It was fortunate that this coincided with a number of HEFCE initiatives in support of libraries that house national research collections and the £1 million project was eventually to be fully funded in this way. Once again, the project was completed to time and on budget and was eventually to allow the relocation of approximately 25 percent of the School's collection from the other floors into the basement. An additional ten years of expansion space had been achieved without the need to go offsite. The Philips Building was also beginning to show its age and technology had impacted on the Library in two ways. Firstly, the organization and processing of loans had changed dramatically, and secondly, there was an increasing need for computer facilities within the Library. One major reading room had been converted to computer facilities some years earlier, and from 2000 on a rolling basis, using further HEFCE funding, a major reorganization and refurbishment programme was initiated, following on from the solution to the Library's long-term storage needs. The majority of the works for modernizing the Library were completed by the end of the summer 2002.

In the summer of 2001 with the prospect of Vernon Square opening shortly, the School was able to relocate the Law Department back to the College Building and to surrender the lease on 46/47 Russell Square. The additional space offered by the Vernon Square campus also meant that the lease on Lynton House could be released. Hence, by 2002 the SOAS estate had been successfully consolidated into two main campuses, held, as had been planned, on a freehold or near-freehold basis.

It should be emphasized that the two main elements of the original Campus Development Plan remained high priorities. The need for additional facilities at Russell Square, especially for research, will continue to grow. As the student body has been spread between the two campuses, congestion is no longer a serious issue. As a result, the Governing Body gave permission in the summer of 2002 for works to the East Block to recommence with the intention that it should provide dedicated research facilities. However, the scheme had been simplified and the contract let on a 'design and build' basis to try to ensure that it was completed to time and on budget. After further delays, work to complete the East Block by early 2004 had finally commenced at the time of publication of this volume.

Not all of the School's space problems were solved by new buildings. Workers in the Square Mile would be amused at the idea that SOAS was short of space for increasing numbers of staff and students. The generous office accommodation enjoyed by professors and other senior academic staff would in the City house a whole department. It is a testament to the performance of the Pro-Director, Professor Christopher Shackle, that one by one these offices were clawed back and either divided into two or used as open-plan offices for support staff. Teaching rooms, too, were often under-utilized with much of the teaching traditionally crammed into timetable slots around lunchtime, Monday to Thursday. The growth in student numbers made it necessary for an increasing number of classes to be distributed across the entire week. This battle is far from over, as in 2002 it was still possible to find a class of students looking for a professor while the professor, having assumed he/she had been allocated the usual room at 11am on Tuesday, stood bemused in front of the wrong class of students.

Partly by good fortune, partly through the ability to take opportunities as they arose, and partly by good planning and management, over a period of eleven years up to 2002 the School had managed to accommodate a dramatic growth in student numbers from 1,200 to 3,500, and 750 residential places had become available for SOAS students without being a financial drain on the School's resources. Along with the acquisition of the second campus at Vernon Square, this has been a very significant achievement. It has, still more, added greatly to the material well-being of the School.

9

'And what should they know of SOAS, who only SOAS know?'

Hugh Baker

Like the Chinese frog at the bottom of the well I have a very restricted view. I came to study Chinese as an undergraduate in 1958, and have stayed here till retirement, more (I insist) through contentment than through inertia. I am asked to attempt an impressionistic biography of the institution over the forty-five years of my acquaintance. I can't say much about its birth and first steps, of course, but luckily Sir Cyril Philips did all that over a quarter of a century ago (see Chapter Two of this volume).

I was a Philips baby. At the beginning of the 1958-59 academic year 'Phil' addressed the assembled School, proudly claiming that it had broken the 'fifty barrier', that is, that there were now over fifty undergraduates enrolled at SOAS. Looking around, it was hard to spot them, except for the conspicuously small handful of women freshers. The men were mainly older. In the case of the British men, virtually all had done their two years of National Service and acquired veneers of maturity and seriousness and deplorable habits such as polishing their shoes every day and wearing white shirts. The postgraduate majority were by definition serious and for the most part invisible, pursuing their research over dusty years, unconcerned by any strictures on urgency to submit and consequently unharrassed by anxious supervisors. One old-timer was said to be in his eleventh year of PhD research and had not yet felt ready for his first supervision.

Apparently not everyone was a *bona fide* student. Not long before, there had been a small rash of spy scandals, but since the School had done its share of training intelligence officers during and after the Second World War, and since presumably a number of the non-British students (and the composition of the student body was no less heterogeneous then than it is today) would have come from similar backgrounds, the outbreak was hardly surprising.

The Junior Common Room was just on the left of the main door of the building, taking up some of the space now posturing as an imposing entrance hall. It was dominated by two enormous round wooden tables which had allegedly been salvaged from the old Finsbury Circus building and by one enormously fat man known as 'Felix'. Felix was certainly not a student. He was rumoured to have been barred from the British Museum reading room for eating oranges in there, so he migrated to SOAS where he spent his days smoking Churchillian cigars and challenging anyone gullible to play chess with him. His favourite gambit was to throw board and pieces into the air when it became apparent that he was likely to lose, accompanied on one occasion by a roared accusation to his opponent: 'You have been PRACTISING!' After a few years a zealous and tolerance-challenged Student Union President had Felix evicted, making the JCR quieter but much less interesting. Almost everyone smoked. There was no bar.

The geography of SOAS was simple and basic. There was just the one building, now known as the Old Building, though the Estates Office is under the delusion that it is called 'College Building' and has (in vain) put up signs to that effect. In the basement were the Senior and Junior Refectories, the tiny Student Union room, the Chinese and Japanese library (dark, chaotic and dirty, books in tottering piles on the floor) and the two squash courts (whose ultimate fate Frank Dabell describes elsewhere in this volume). The main Library occupied the right hand side of the ground floor and the reading room shared the left-hand side with the JCR. The Senior Common Room was on the first floor where now is the Director's office; the Director and Secretary had rooms above the main door where the General Office is; the Registry was next to them; and what is now the Staff Common Room was part of the Far East Department. Apart from the Common Rooms and the Directorial suite, much of the rest of the building was unfinished. The walls were bare breeze blocks, the electrical wiring hung swaying in the draughts from the ill-fitting plywood doors, and there was only one telephone per department, located in the office of the department secretary with an extension through to the Head. The medieval moat which surrounds the Old Building was dry even in those far off days.

The hierarchy within the School was very clear. The senior officers were the Director, Secretary, and eight Heads of Departments. Professor Cyril Philips had been promoted to the Directorship only the previous year. It cannot have been easy to follow the twenty year rule of his predecessor, and not all of his erstwhile academic peers within the School were disposed to give him unstinting support, but he proved to have vision and a toughness and quickness in committee which enabled him to realize it. The Secretary, Lt.-Col. H. Moyse-Bartlett, was as military-looking as the retained use of his title would suggest, and he worked with a precision and efficiency which found few detractors, while he was known to be kind and scrupulously fair to those who sought his help. For most students, though, dealings at School level meant going to see the Registrar, Miss Kathleen Wooding. She was a delight whose big brown eyes and dark brown plummy-accented voice exuded maternal love for all her flock.

The Heads of Departments held life-time appointments which came with certain named chairs, and they had considerable power. It could be very bad news to oppose or fall out with one's Head, though for the most part there was not an oppressive atmosphere in departments and abuse of power was more a matter of failure to consult or share decision-making rather than vindictive authoritarianism. The contribution of some of the Heads to the development of the School has been described by Philips as 'immeasurable'. My own Colossus was Professor Walter Simon, Professor of Chinese and Head of the Far East Department, a post he had held since 1936. In my first year I attended his lectures on Sinology and on Bibliography, outpourings of distilled knowledge which my then level of understanding was quite incapable of accommodating. He read Chinese, Manchu, Japanese and Tibetan, and was cast in a mould of scholarship to which few could aspire. Some years ago I was reminiscing about him with his son, Professor Harry Simon, who told me that he once found his father reading a book in Hungarian and asked him how many European languages he could read – the quiet reply after pause for thought was 'Well, all of them, I suppose'. He commanded great respect and I did not sense any resentment from the department staff against his authority. Yet in later years I discovered that one of the academics in his department had been personally instructed to undertake a transposition of Simon's *A Beginners' Chinese-English Dictionary* from Mandarin into Cantonese, a laborious task which must have taken many months (if not years) to do, and which, though completed satisfactorily (I saw the card index), was never sent to a publisher. Such an order would hardly be issued today, nor meekly followed if issued.

The teaching staff who were next down the pecking order were an interesting mixture of brilliant minds, dedicated pedagogues, and of course a few less committed or less gifted individuals 'by aventure y-falle in felawshipe'. These 'sondry folk' included a number who persistently challenged their livers, a lecturer who always cancelled classes when England were playing at Twickenham or Lords, assorted eccentrics of a more or less dangerous kind, and the Phoneticians, generally thought to be harmlessly batty owing to their habit of walking down the corridors mouthing improbable sounds to themselves. None were as remiss in their observance of duty as one of my predecessors, Sir Reginald Johnston, Professor of Chinese (1931-37), who lived in the Hebrides and was said to have appeared in the School only once a year (his former position as tutor to the boy emperor of China had perhaps made him somewhat 'imperious'). Some of the teachers were nominal in the sense that they 'taught' subjects for which there were no students. Professor Harry Shorto, whose subject was Old Mon, is widely believed never to have had a student in all the years from joining the staff in 1953 until 1984 when he retired, but in 1985 I met a woman in Australia who told me that this was not true and that she was in fact his one and only student: 'I was in his room one day, when the phone rang. He picked it up and without waiting to hear who was calling said "I cannot speak at the moment. I am teaching", then put the phone down with great pride.'

SOAS was small and it was friendly. Institutional life was relaxed and relatively free from outside pressures or financial constraint. A hierarchy there most certainly was, demarcation lines extending to the toilets (the staff toilets actually sported unchained nail brushes, I discovered when I daringly sneaked in for a peep) as well as to the refectories and common rooms, but red-tape barely existed, and staff and students could not fail to know each other quite well, just as the small size of the undergraduate body meant that everyone knew everyone else regardless of what subjects they were studying.

By 1960 when I found myself President of the Student Union, numbers had grown to the point where it was possible to organize quite a range of social activities, with twice-yearly dances (of the 'Strictly Ballroom' type, French-chalk on the floor), debates, a film society, and the Union's first newsletter *KIP*, the name, suggestive of a certain lethargy, in fact deriving from the SOAS motto **Knowledge Is Power**. This upsurge in activity was helped by the abolition of National Service, which meant an influx of school-leavers who were more eager and 'clubbable' than the 'veterans'.

'Worshipping his ancestral tablets, after taking his degree'

In the spring of 1961 there took place an extraordinary 'Staff-Student Tournament' comprising a package of chess matches, bridge, debating, squash, and a long-distance run from Hampstead Whitestone Pond to the School, where one of the staff was so late finishing that it was suspected he had slipped in for a glass of liver medicine on the way. The battered silver cup, donated by Mr John Burton-Page, Lecturer in Hindi and Nepali, was won by the students, but like other more heavily publicized trophies it seems to have disappeared and the police were not alerted. The squash courts, our one tangible sporting asset, had always been well used by both staff and students, the whipping backhand of Professor (of Persian) Ann Lambton striking terror into her opponents of whatever age or gender right through until her retirement in 1979.

At Christmas there was a joint staff-student concert with the star turn being Dr Cyril Birch (now a Professor Emeritus of the University of California, Berkeley) who delivered uncannily accurate renditions of Tom Lehrer's comic (only later would they be called satirical) songs accompanying himself at the piano, while Miss Nora Shane (then Secretary to the Far East Department and Miss Angela Faragher (Near and Middle East Department Secretary) performed spirited duets at the same instrument, and Mr Jack Carnochan (now Professor Emeritus of Phonetics) had a go at conjuring tricks. One year we put on a comic play instead. There was always a full house. The SOAS gods were in their various heavens and most things seemed right with the world.

But an expanding student body and more staff meant a need for more accommodation. A fourth floor was added to the Old Building in 1961, houses in Woburn Square and buildings further away in Fitzroy Square, Howland Street and Covent Garden were pressed into service, and the Library began a series of inconvenient and sometimes near disastrous sojournings wherever it could find space (at one site near Tottenham Court Road there were buckets placed between the stacks to catch water from the leaking roof). As the 1960s went on there were those who became alert to the effect which growth and dispersal were having on the comfortable family intimacy we had enjoyed. In an effort to shore up a sense of collegiate unity Dr Guy Atkins (Lecturer in Bantu Languages), Dr Ben Segal (Reader in Aramaic and Syriac) and Dr Harold Blakemore (Education Officer) joined forces with the Student Union to run regular 'Supper Lectures', mostly with speakers of some eminence invited in from outside. For one or two years these attracted large mixed audiences, but support fell away and there were no follow-up initiatives.

It did not seem very significant at the time, but in retrospect perhaps the event which confirmed the setting in of a slow drift to polarization of the School was the concerted effort by the Student Union to win control of the squash courts, packing a General Meeting and voting staff members off the Squash Club Committee. And during the 1960s the Union, in keeping with the spirit of the times, became increasingly politicized, first shedding its homely social club image and then moving to active confrontation with the School establishment in the heady days of the Paris riots and the troubles at LSE and elsewhere.

In the mid 1960s I was away conducting fieldwork and then writing up, so that my exposure to the changes taking place was quite limited. When I joined the staff in October 1967 it was not immediately apparent that anything was different. Indeed, the manner of my joining was very much in tune with the informal SOAS I had known as a student. The day after my PhD viva I had been called in by Lt.-Col. Moyse-Bartlett who congratulated me and asked if I would like to have a job teaching Chinese. My affirmative answer clinched the matter; the whole process of becoming employed as Lecturer in Chinese took about five minutes from non-application to end of non-interview, and to the best of my knowledge no committee had been consulted, no advertisement had been issued, and no question as to whether the School could afford to employ me had been asked. Perhaps Moyse-Bartlett was 'demob-happy' in the last few months of his Secretaryship before he was succeeded by his equally efficient deputy John Bracken. If so, he was not happy to the extent that he overspent: for those who like to gasp over money, my starting salary was £1,740 plus £60 London Allowance.

Nor was any change to be seen in the invitation soon afterwards to join the staff dining club, the 49 Club, which had been founded in 1949 by forty-nine members. I was first asked if I would be prepared to be nominated, then my name was put up for election, and there being no blackballs deployed against me I duly became a member. We dined once a term, and no speeches were allowed. Only males from the teaching and senior administrative staff were permitted to join, but political correctness had not yet been invented. We ate and drank well at moderate cost, and a seating plan ensured that no-one could sit next to members of the same department, so that here was a chance to break out of the narrow circle set by the demands of everyday work and to resume collegiate life of a kind at least. (Within a few short years most of the exclusivity of this bastion was evaporated, first by letting women dine as guests, then by throwing open membership to women, and finally by permitting would-be members to apply rather than wait to be asked, but it continues to set a rare example of cross-departmental socializing.)

But things were indeed changing, if grudgingly on the part of some. It is not that the School had been completely insensitive to the problems or the need for change, some of which in any case had been driven from the top. Phil was busily expanding the scope of our subject-cover in the social sciences as well as our overall student population, and he and others could not have been blind to the functional relationships between numbers and systems. Professor Denis Twitchett had brokered a deal with thirty secondary schools around the country to start teaching Chinese with the support of his Department, aiming both to increase numbers and to improve standards. Robin Saville and Harold Blakemore as Education Officers had begun to spread news of SOAS and its studies to schools nationwide. But many were reluctant to move from the old ways of doing things, often for fear that the new must be inferior to the established, and there was a genuine bewilderment that students should want a say in the running of the institution when not a few staff themselves wanted only to get on with their research. It seems shocking now that at the height of the tense relations between School and students one professor refused to supervise a research student until he had shaved off his beard, deemed to be unsightly: perhaps even more shocking to report that the student complied.

The institutional soul-searching which went on as a response to the trauma of 'student revolt' in 1968 focused upon what was possibly not one of the least of our shortcomings – attention to teaching quality. Lecturers were encouraged to attend sessions on 'How to…' delivered by senior academics whose own thoughts had been hastily assembled from the previously unpondered depths of their experience. I remember the lecture on 'How to give a slide lecture', marred by slides inserted upside down, back to front and sometimes in the wrong order, leaving the audience unsure whether we were being taught by 'negative example' or whether, as was strongly rumoured, the speaker was being made to suffer for having had a disagreement with the technician beforehand. The services of the Institute of Education were called upon, and some of us went for courses in teaching technique which lasted for one or even as long as two days. It all seemed rather ludicrous and was certainly inadequate, but I can date a new attitude to the planning and implementation of courses and to the necessity for better textbooks from that time, and I firmly believe that considerable improvements eventually resulted. Students were invited onto various School committees as members or observers, addressing (albeit reluctantly) one of the most vociferous demands which had been made. It is indicative of the resistance to this step that even now student membership is only just being implemented on some committees, though the long delay is partly to be blamed on periods of student apathy in the intervening thirty years.

'The tumult and the shouting' of the late 1960s died down soon enough, but the problems of trying to fit more and more people into our limited space remained. The next major conflict was not internal, nor was it strictly speaking academic at all. For some years there had existed a dream of a major extension to the School buildings and by the mid-1960s a design was ready. Unfortunately, to build the design would require road closures and the demolition of some houses and other buildings in Woburn Square, and the protests against this 'destruction of Bloomsbury' were loudly heard on all sides. The Anthropology Department, which used some of the threatened houses, knew well that they were not prime stock, the floors and the walls having parted company to the extent that demolition would have been unnecessary in a year or two, while one of the threatened treasures was a garage with a corrugated iron roof, and the other an undistinguished Victorian church. Still, it was undeniable that there was going to be impingement on one of Bloomsbury's most distinctive features and the protesters were well connected and nearly carried the day. Phil was magnificent in leadership (or monstrous if you were a protester): he cajoled and blustered, wheedled and reasoned, and finally, by the time it came to the showdown meeting of Convocation in Senate House, he had mustered a very large number of SOAS staff to attend and vote for the scheme to go ahead. Work started in 1970. Without qualm I had marched with Phil, and would do so again, but I confess to feeling nauseated when I saw how the stumps of the great plane trees that had to be felled bled red sap.

The New Building (properly and deservedly named the Philips Building now) was opened in 1973, complete with a state of the art purpose-built Library. Suddenly conditions were comfortable. Where before 1973 I shared a small unplastered room on the third floor with two colleagues, running down two floors to the department office if a phone call should become absolutely necessary and popping in there several times a day to ask if there had been any calls for me, now I had a well-appointed room just as large to myself, and I had a telephone too.

The School had shown considerable unity over the Convocation vote, it was all under the same roof again, and now we could go forward as one. True, the New Building was not very conducive to socializing, with its long corridors lined with closed doors and the separation of departments on different floors, but any floor plan would have had some such drawback. What we found, in fact, was that we had contained the bodies but had not recaptured the family spirit, and it was not really reasonable to expect that we should. We had entered, indeed are still in, a stage of development where we were too big to be small and not yet big enough to be big: we may have reached institutional puberty forty years ago but we had still not attained adulthood. The transition period has been uncomfortable and muddled, but that is generally in the nature of growing up and I see no reason to look to blame either the conservatives or the reformers if we have not always had immediate correct responses. There were those who advocated radical reorganization as the answer, but most of us accepted growth by piecemeal accumulation rather than by planned development, every now and then shaking the bits in the hope that they would resettle into an efficient pattern within the familiar framework.

One change which eventually came about as a result of events in the early 1970s was the abolition of the powerful, permanent tenure of Heads of Department. In at least two cases in quick succession there had been strong suspicion that the non-renewal of a probationary lecturer's contract had been occasioned by personal or political animosity on the part of the Heads concerned and that academic merit had been ignored or played down. I knew one of the lecturers well and believed at the time and still do that the Head's motivation was at best dubious. Protests saved neither probationer, but there was heated debate in committees and eventually a Committee of Four (variously known as the 'Four Wise Men' and the 'Gang of Four') senior academics who were not Heads of Department was set up to vet all probationary appointments and to confirm or reject the formerly unquestionable recommendations of the Head of Department. Even when Headship was decoupled from named chairs and allowed to rotate amongst department staff, the Gang of Four continued to pronounce its verdicts, not always agreeing with the Heads' judgements. In some cases the Gang, just like the Heads, got it wrong, but it was generally agreed that the new procedures stood a better chance of being fair and they were in place until the mid-1990s when a formal Promotions Committee was set up. The change away from permanent Heads was almost sabotaged when it was discovered that the tying of Headships to named chairs was actually enshrined in the School's Charter, and for some time Heads were required to be called by the clumsy term 'Acting Heads', a device reflected po-faced in the School Calendars from 1985-86 to 1989-90. Standing in for a colleague on research leave I gloried for a year in the title 'Temporary Acting Head of Department' – not one reflecting overweening power, I think.

After being known by numbers for two years of National Service and by personal names at secondary school, my generation had relished being called 'Mr Smith' and 'Miss Carruthers', but in what seemed to me a curious inversion students now wanted to be called 'Chris' and 'Freda'. It was as though this would somehow compensate for the loss of individuality in the larger class sizes. And as student numbers grew, so inexorably the School's administrative and teaching staff expanded. In 1958 we had managed to run SOAS with a Secretary assisted by one Deputy and one Assistant, a Registrar, and an Accountant with one Assistant Accountant. If 'clerks' (as they were then known) and technicians were counted in, the entire central administrative force came to a total of twenty people. There are more than six times as many now. Student numbers have risen over the same period more than fourfold; academic staff in administrative roles have increased. In 1967 the office of Dean was created as lieutenant to the Director, the title being changed in 1979 to Pro-Director, and in the course of time more Deans and Pro-Directors were added to the list, each with designated responsibilities for different areas of the School's work. Committees and sub-committees multiplied (from thirteen in 1960 to more than forty now). In the same period, full-time teaching staff numbers have risen by less than 50 percent from 172 to 233. It is not difficult to see why we have had to become more bureaucratic and less particularist.

As recounted in Richard Rathbone's chapter earlier, Phil was succeeded as Director by Professor C. D. (Jeremy) Cowan in 1976, just as University funding began to shrink drastically. Expansive optimism gave way to anxious pessimism, and within four years we were facing severe cuts. Unable to support a teaching staff of over 200, a massive scheme of early retirements was implemented. Older members of staff were encouraged to apply to retire, and when the books still would not balance, increasing moral pressure was put on anyone over the age of 57 to think of applying 'for the good of the School'. The axe fell on approximately a quarter of the staff, but it fell arbitrarily according to age rather than in a planned fashion. Most of the retirements came in 1981-83, some departments which had had a high proportion of senior staff suddenly being stripped of their brightest stars, and the loss of experience, academic authority, and unique language and discipline skills dealt a severe blow to the institution's balance and morale.

To try to impose order on the situation, the first of the big internal enquiries into the running of the School was set up. The Working Party on Longer-term Development was chaired by Dr (later Professor) Malcolm Yapp, and as part of its work it embarked on an exhaustive programme of interviews with every member of the teaching staff in an attempt to understand what was the irreducible minimum complement below which the ability of SOAS to operate effectively would be called into question. As a member of the Working Party I am left now with only the haziest recollection of months of interminable talking and note-taking, but shining through the mist remains a sense of the commitment and integrity of so many, leavened by the mendacious creativity of the few (one colleague claimed to teach fifteen hours a week, but only came into the School on Thursdays). The Yapp Report was published in 1982 entertaining all with its categorization of languages and disciplines as American Indian tribes, its insistence on half-posts and its advocacy of 'watching briefs', garments designed to conceal the naked gaps in our academic coverage. Within only weeks of the appearance of the Report, Academic Board approved a new post not envisaged in it, a matter of great frustration to the compilers but a comforting reminder to the reactionaries that SOAS had not yet totally succumbed to bureaucratic procedure. The Yapp Report was followed by others at short intervals over the next twenty years, some of them accepted, some of them ignored, and some of them accepted and then ignored. It was not until 2002 under the impetus of a new broom wielded by Director Professor Colin Bundy that the report of a working party set up to look at the organizational structure of the School came to be fully implemented, departments being subsumed under three faculties.

In 1958 the student body was heavily postgraduate, but for the next thirty years the proportion of undergraduates steadily climbed, until in the 1990s government policies made it financially beneficial to increase postgraduate numbers again, particularly by attracting students onto taught Masters courses. Meanwhile, in the mid-1970s we changed from Finals-based degrees to Course Unit degrees, and this encouraged the growth of joint honours degrees such as Japanese and Economics or Development Studies and Social Anthropology. Such degrees proved very popular but the large number of permutations which could be taken by students meant a greatly lengthened examination period in order to accommodate them all, and with examinations at the end of each year, the teaching year was shortened accordingly. An abortive attempt to bring all London University terms into line meant that in the early 1990s we changed from our traditional 10-10-9 week year to a 12-12-6 week year, ostensibly clawing back a teaching week, but in fact 12-week terms were deemed to be too long and tiring, so that each of them was broken up by a mid-term Reading Week, losing yet more teaching time. To some extent, then, the improvements which have been made in teaching and in textbooks have been offset by the reduction in classroom hours.

Nor has the life of the student become any easier. I received a full maintenance grant of £90 a term when I was a student, and with careful husbandry and working every vacation I could live adequately well. Now most students have no financial support, on the contrary they have to pay student fees and in many cases take out loans to cover maintenance. Working part-time during term-time has become a necessity for some, and some even attempt what is logically and in practice impossible by trying to hold down full-time jobs. The quality of our students has not gone down, but their attitudes to university education have changed. They expect more of us and they tend to see their degree principally in terms of an essential stepping stone to a career rather than as a matter of improving education or of promoting scholarship. For many teachers it is incomprehensible that a student should complain about being required to attend a background course on Chinese history and culture on the grounds that 'I am going to be a journalist/ trader/lawyer/diplomat/banker dealing with China and the course is not relevant'. And apparently such a student cannot comprehend that attending the course might make for a better journalist/etc. Yet we have been at all times fortunate in attracting a majority of serious students who come to study rather than play, so if the change in attitude is to be deplored it should be tempered with a Ciceronian 'O tempora, O mores'.

All around SOAS sits London jealously seducing the society of our souls, and we lead an impoverished collegiate life accordingly. Twenty years ago a brave group of us tried to organize a SOAS Ball, but months of planning and proselytization produced so negative a response that we had to abort the idea. The 49 Club has gone through some very lean times, and the more recently founded Women's Dining Club has managed to survive too, but neither would dare to try to meet more frequently. We are a diurnal beast. But we are not anti-social and we are not obscure or without reputation. Since I first went abroad as a research student under the aegis of the School I have been struck by how well thought of we are and how much looked up to as a Centre of Excellence (forgive the jargon, but it is appropriate here). Abroad perhaps more so than in Britain to be a member of SOAS is to be a greater person than just oneself.

We may ourselves be aware of many constraints and compromises, but nowhere else is there such a concentration of high expertise on Asia and Africa and we have not been ungenerous in making available our learning to others. From the 1960s onwards we have participated in programmes to disseminate our knowledge to wider audiences. Under the auspices of the old Extra-Mural Division, for years headed brilliantly by the quiet benignity of Ted O'Connor and Stuart Simmonds (Professor of South East Asian Languages and Literatures), we used to send lecturers out to schools and societies all over the country, and many of us cut our lecturing teeth on sixth forms in Cumbria, historical societies in Bedfordshire and Council for Education in World Citizenship groups in Norwich or Rochester. I once spent a bewildering afternoon lecturing on the Chinese family to a group of unmarried mothers in a national weekend refuge home in Somerset improbably funded by the Greater London Council. There was an annual tour of West Country schools on which a small circus of us would go, and great fun it was too. By the 1970s we had begun receiving Leverhulme money to run one-term Schoolteacher Fellowship Programmes, bringing the cream of the country's sixth form teachers to the School for intensive training in one or other of our areas of expertise, then sending them back to infect their pupils with the enthusiasm and knowledge they had gained.

Later the External Services Division, then the Language Centre and the Briefing Office took over the extra-mural role. We have run trade briefings for Shell, language courses for Swire & Sons, study packs on Korea for schools, cultural background courses for the Swedish, German and Irish governments, intensive language training for our own Foreign and Commonwealth Office, not to mention the part-time, intensive and diploma language courses that hundreds of non-degree students a year take in the Language Centre. We have helped with interpreting in police stations and immigration offices, prepared reports for international conferences, given expert evidence in courts, recorded sound-bites for radio and television current affairs programmes, written and fronted television documentaries, contributed articles and copy for newspapers, been consulted on selling hamburgers, biscuits and alcoholic drinks, written national anthems for newly independent countries, and even advised on what Chinese name Marks & Spencer should adopt when opening in Beijing. Such activities are a significant and relevant aspect of our academic work, and they succeed in spreading our learning to many more than we could reach through our intra-mural teaching and learned publications alone. We now have a professionally staffed Interface Office to promote and facilitate this kind of activity, and the hope is that it will grow to be of financial benefit to the School and to those who participate as well as being valuable to our customers.

Like it or not we have become much less isolated from the world outside our walls, and we cannot ignore the pressures and demands of the society within which we operate. We may be an exotic and skilful piper but we are paid by the state and the state calls its favourite tunes while subjecting us to rigorous pipe inspections to ensure that we rehearse and play (research and teach) to standard. We used to decide our own programmes with little regard to what the students wanted, but we now are heavily dependent financially upon attracting and keeping student audiences, and it would be as impolitic to ignore student preference as it would be to offer unsuitable goods for consumption by any other market customer. After-concert services include professional careers advice and a burgeoning alumni association.

What then of the changes in forty-five years? We have certainly become more professional in our teaching and procedures, more regulation conscious, more responsive to change, more 'standardized'. As we have grown bigger we have had to forgo some of the personal touches which made SOAS so cosy. We used to have a wealth of eccentrics, such as Felix, or Mr Gordon Downer who once wrote back from study leave asking for a water buffalo and some corrugated iron with which to pay his linguistic informants in Cambodia, or Mr Cyril Jones the Head Porter who would from time to time astonish visitors and make the entrance hall resound with his sudden imitation of a trumpet, an effect achieved with much lip-pursing and redness of face. There was Professor David Lang (Caucasian Studies) who after his customary heavy lunch never stayed at Academic Board for more than a few minutes, but who never failed to bow deeply to the Chair as he withdrew; Professor Angus Graham (Classical Chinese) who never attended Academic Board at all and who, when he retired, simply decamped leaving everything including pipe and slippers in his room; and Professor 'Bobby' Robins (Linguistics) who was an excellent extempore speaker but who would only lecture from notes carefully timed to the second and checked against his watch page by page as he spoke. Professor D. S. 'Storm' Rice (Islamic Art and Archaeology) was wont to slip the odd slide of a belly-dancer into his more serious presentations, whether to wake himself or his audience was not known; Professor Christoph von Fürer-Haimendorf (Anthropology) believed in 'saying it with flowers', to the great profit of the florists it is said; and there was Mr S. Yanada (Japanese) who could never understand why so many students found it funny that his textbook included as an everyday phrase 'There is a cat behind the dictionary'.

We still have 'characters' of course, but their impact has become less as the School has got bigger. Difficulty in making humane exceptions is the downside of strict regulations made for the greater benefit of the majority. Loss of individuality and the personal touch is the price which is paid for the objective anonymity of the examinee's number. 'And a good thing too', say the purists, but the purists may never win the entire field. I remember a wonderful teacher who never published, an awful teacher who published wonderful writings, excellent teachers and researchers who hated administrative work – their careers would be harder, perhaps untenable in the SOAS to which we are being so directly steered by the bureaucratic forces of engrossment and universalization. Yet my forty-five years with the School tell me that we have managed to hold on with remarkable tenacity to the basic decencies of the civilized life, and just as we have sidestepped the deepest of the muddy puddles of dissent and internal feud so we have always stopped short of the heartless iciness of regulated conformity.

'He who can, does. He who cannot, teaches' was one of Shaw's cheapest jibes. Well, in forty-five years I have never lost the certainty that I am living in a community of highest scholarship amongst colleagues at all levels who can and who do and who will go on trying. I cannot believe that we are incapable of holding onto our humanity even while we grow bigger, and I see no possibility of ever being other than proud to have been part of this School.

Appendices

Notes on contributors

David Arnold, BA (Exeter), DPhil (Sussex), came to SOAS from the University of Lancaster in 1988 as Professor of the History of South Asia. He was Head of the Department of History (1992-96) and Pro-Director for Research (1999-2002).

Hugh Baker, BA, PhD (London), was a student at SOAS, whose academic staff he joined in 1967 as Lecturer in Chinese, becoming Professor of Chinese in 1990. He was Head of the Contemporary China Institute (1981-86), twice Head of the Department of the Far East/East Asia (1987-94, 1997-2002), and Dean of Interface (2001-03).

Terence J. Byres, MA (Aberdeen), BLitt (Glasgow), joined the SOAS staff in 1962 as Research Fellow in Economics with reference to South Asia, becoming Professor of Political Economy in 1992. He was Head of the Department of Economics (1990-94), and since his retirement in 1998 has been a Professorial Research Associate in the Departments of Development Studies and Economics.

Frank Dabell, BA (York), came to SOAS from City University in 1993 as School Secretary, then Secretary and Registrar until 2002. He is now Clerk to the Governing Body.

J.D.Y. Peel, MA (Oxon), PhD, DLit (London), FBA, came to SOAS from the University of Liverpool in 1989 as Professor of Anthropology and Sociology with reference to Africa. He was Dean of Undergraduate Studies (1991-94).

Sir Cyril Philips, MA, PhD (London), DLitt, LLD, was Professor of Oriental History and Director of SOAS from 1957 until 1976. He was the author of the short history *The School of Oriental and African Studies, University of London, 1917-1967: An Introduction* (SOAS, 1967) and an autobiography *Beyond the Ivory Tower* (1995).

Richard Rathbone, BA, PhD (London), FRHistS, joined the SOAS staff in 1969 as Lecturer in the Contemporary History of Africa, becoming Professor of Modern African History in 1995 until his early retirement in 2003. He was Chair of the Centre of African Studies (1985-89) and Dean of Postgraduate Studies (1991-95).

Rosemary Seton, BA (Wales), DipEd (Reading), MA, DipArchiveStudies (London), FRHS, joined the staff of the SOAS Library from the India Office Library and Records in 1980 as Archivist. In 2002 she became Keeper of Archives and Special Collections.

Christopher Shackle, BA, DipSocAnthrop, BLitt (Oxon), PhD (London), FBA, joined SOAS in 1966 as a Fellow in Indian Studies, becoming Professor of the Modern Languages of South Asia in 1985. He was Head of the Department of South Asia (1983-87), Pro-Director for Academic Affairs (1997-2002) and Pro-Director (2002-03).

Keith Webster, BSc (Loughborough), MLib (Wales), FCLIP, FRGS, Hon FCLIP, joined SOAS from the University of Newcastle in 1999 as Librarian and Director of Information Services. Since 2002 he has been Director of Information Services and Strategy.

Principal office holders 1967-2002

Chairs of Governing Body

1960-75	Viscount Radcliffe
1975-80	Lord Gore-Booth
1980-86	Lord Greenhill
1986-90	Lord MacLehose
1990-98	Sir Robert Wade-Gery
1999-present	Jonathan Taylor

Directors

1957-76	Professor Sir Cyril Philips (Vice-Chancellor 1973-76)
1976-89	Professor C.D. Cowan
1989-96	Sir Michael McWilliam
1996-2000	Sir Timothy Lankester
2001-present	Professor Colin Bundy (Director & Principal)

Deans and Pro-Directors

1967-73	Christoph von Fürer-Haimendorf (Dean, Acting Director 1973-76)
1973-82	Stuart Simmonds (Dean, then Pro-Director from 1981)
1982-84	Charles Bawden
1984-85	Adrian Mayer
1985-92	John Wansbrough
1992-96	Robert Taylor
1997-2003	Christopher Shackle (Acting Director January-April 2001)

Principal Academic Office Holders

Dean of Students

1973-76   C.D. Cowan

Deans of Studies

1977-78   Roland Oliver

1978-81   Humphrey Fisher

1981-86   Malcolm Yapp

Deans of Undergraduate Studies (Pro-Director from 1997)

1986-87   Ian Raeside

1987-91   Harry Norris

1991-94   J.D.Y. Peel

1994   Caroline Dinwiddy

1995-97   David Taylor

1997-98   Julia Leslie

Senior Tutors

1973-77   Roland Oliver

1977-82   George Milner

1982-86   Ian Raeside

Deans of Postgraduate Studies (Pro-Director from 1997)

1986-89   Richard Gray

1989-91   Graham Chapman

1991-95   Richard Rathbone

1995-96   Laurence Harris

1996-98   Geoffrey King

Pro-Director for Taught Courses

1998-2002   David Taylor

Dean of Special Courses (of Continuing Education from 1992)

1991-94   Tony Allan

Dean of Languages

1995-97   Graham Furniss

Dean of Research (Pro-Directors from 1997)

1996-98   Laurence Harris

1998-2002   David Arnold

Secretaries

To 1967   Lt.-Col. H. Moyse-Bartlett

1967-80   John Bracken

1981-83   Colin Moore

1983-87   Edward O'Connor

1987-93   David Edwards

1993-2002   Frank Dabell (Secretary & Registrar from 2001)

Librarians

1950-72   J.D. Pearson

1972-78   Barry Bloomfield

1978-83   V.T.H. Parry

1983-92   Barbara Burton

1992-98   Mary Auckland

1999-2002   Keith Webster (Librarian and Director of Information Services)